Syrup Pails
and Gopher Tails

Syrup Pails and Gopher Tails

Memories of the One~Room School

John C Charyk

Western Producer Prairie Books

Saskatoon, Saskatchewan

Cover and book design by John Luckhurst
Cover painting by Don Frache

Printed and bound in Canada by Modern Press ⟿ 1
Saskatoon, Saskatchewan.

The publisher acknowledges the support
received for this publication from the Canada
Council.

Western Producer Prairie Books publications
are produced and manufactured in the middle
of western Canada by a unique publishing
venture owned by a group of prairie farmers
who are members of Saskatchewan Wheat
Pool. From the first book published in 1954, a
reprint of a serial originally carried in the
weekly newspaper, *The Western Producer,* to
the book before you now, the tradition of
providing enjoyable and informative reading for
all Canadians is continued.

Canadian Cataloguing in Publication Data

Charyk, John C., 1908-
    Syrup pails and gopher tails

    Bibliography: p. 137
    Includes index.
    ISBN 0-88833-115-0 (bound).

    1. Rural schools — Prairie Provinces —
History. 2. Prairie Provinces — History —
1905-1945.* I. Title.
LB1568.C3C49 1983   372.9712   C83-091399-8

Contents

Preface

The story of the one-room school is an exciting one of initiative, determination, disappointment, and courage. Yet it is a short story, encompassing a period of only seventy-five years. The schools came into being by the beginning of the twentieth century as a necessary line of cultural defense for the future; grew steadily with each new wave of immigration; flourished between 1932 and 1942; started to decline rapidly after World War II; and, by 1965, disappeared almost entirely.

Even so, they have served our country well. What took place in these small country schools was instrumental in cementing our democratic way of life. It can be said that Canada's future was written on the blackboards of the little rural schoolhouses.

Syrup Pails and Gopher Tails is filled with personal memories, in both word and picture, of what it was like to attend the one-room school whether you were a student, the teacher, a parent, or a school official. It portrays the very life and spirit of these once proud institutions of learning.

Through the cooperation and kindness of interested people, corporations, teachers' organizations, and archives, this volume is enriched with a wealth of rare pictures of former times which yield their historical information at a single glance. Good camera testaments of activities in the one-room school during the past half century have been few and far between. Cameras were not always to be had, and if one was available, the picture-takers were often unfamiliar with the techniques required. People taking snapshots were sure to focus the camera in the direction of their own darlings and miss the important part of the scene. A time exposure, the means of taking indoor pictures in those early days, rarely turned out successfully on Christmas concert night, so the children were photographed in their costumes outside the schoolhouse. However, if the weather at the time was too cold for wearing the skimpy crepe paper costumes, the pictures were taken in spring or early summer, or when a camera was again available.

History is a branch of knowledge that records and explains past events. But more than that, it conjures up feelings of what it was like in a day and age not our own. One of the aims of *Syrup Pails and Gopher Tails* is to provide such an experience by allowing the one-room school generation to speak in their own unique way.

School lunches, like this one in the Bienfait S.D. (Bienfait, Saskatchewan), have always been an important part of the day.

Chapter One

First Impressions

Today Is the Day

Today's child has been well prepared for the time he enters school and starts grade one. Many have attended a nursery school, a play school, or kindergarten or have at least taken part in three- or four-day familiarization sessions in the latter part of June. Through such experiences the beginner knows something about classroom routine and discipline. He also has at least an inkling of what is expected of him, how to get along with his classmates, and why he is attending school. The majority of beginners in the early days of the rural school had no such introductions or advantages. They came in "cold." These tots entered school for the first time completely ignorant of what went on in a classroom. It probably was as dramatic an experience for the beginner as it would be for an adult to land on the planet Mars and be told to fend for himself in the strange environment among its singular inhabitants.

That is just the way I felt when I started school in the Laggan S.D. 1063 (Lake Louise, Alberta) one September day in 1913. I had absolutely no idea of what school was all about, nor of what I was expected to do. To make matters worse, I understood very little English and spoke even less. The experience was so traumatic that although it occurred over sixty-six years ago, it is still as fresh in my mind as if it had happened just yesterday.

I knew something was in the wind when after my fifth birthday in July my parents began to give more attention to me than to my younger brother and sister, Nick and Mary. Heretofore it had been the reverse. In addition, when a parcel arrived from the T. Eaton Co. Limited, it contained more clothes for me than for any other member of the family. This was also unusual. I was told I was going to start school. The way that my parents talked about "school" it seemed to be something that was going to be very important for me now, and even more so in the future. All this was beyond my comprehension, but as long as this incessant talk about school didn't affect me for the moment, I didn't worry.

However, one morning things changed dramatically. I was roused earlier than usual, and although it wasn't Sunday, my mother gave me an extra good washing and helped me put on my new clothes. I was told today was the day I was starting school.

If school was going to be such a good thing for me, why were my parents exhibiting so much sadness? Mother was weeping fitfully while my father, who usually never displayed his emotions, hastily wiped a few tears from his eyes. His voice sounded husky as he placed his trembling hand on my head, mumbled something, and hurriedly left for work. For the first time this "school" business had me worried. There must be something sinister about it, or why were my parents so distressed? I seemed to be the pawn in this affair so I decided to be wary.

Soon after my father had left, one of the railway section hands appeared at our house. Apparently he had been delegated by my father to take me to school and register me. My mother couldn't speak English very well so it would have been useless for her to go; and my father was too conscientious to use company time to accompany me, hence the substitute.

As we were leaving the house, my mother kept repeating, "Be good in school! Be good in school! And then she broke into tears again. All this display of emotions disturbed and frustrated me. Besides, I couldn't make any sense out of being "good in school" when I didn't even know how to be *bad* in school. I was more confused than ever by this time. However, I felt somewhat consoled when my escort took my hand tenderly in his big, rough and calloused one and said, "You come mit me!" So we set out for I knew not what. I looked back once, and my mother was still in the doorway looking very forlorn. I felt like giving my guide the slip and running back to her, but he must have anticipated my move for his hand tightened and held mine like a vice. I was a prisoner.

In no time we had walked beyond the boundaries of my usual haunts, so there was much to interest me. My "friend" didn't talk to me and seemed to be preoccupied with his own problem, probably that of meeting and talking to such an important person as the teacher. His self-absorption gave me an opportunity to study his unusual appearance. I remember he was short, stooped, bowlegged. But the part about him that intrigued me most was the waxed handlebar mustache that swept across his wrinkled face. Every once in a while he would use his free hand to twist the ends of this mustache — rather proudly, I thought. In after years I would have said he was a typical cossack. He probably was.

I soon realized we were approaching a small white building that seemed to be all windows on one side. It was then that he spoke to me for the first time. He pointed to the fairy-tale cottage and said, "School!" I smiled and felt pleased. School didn't appear to be such a bad place after all.

The moment we reached it, he knocked on the door and we waited for what seemed a long time before a pleasant-looking woman appeared. My escort rather nervously and hesitantly talked to her in broken English. She then asked him a number of questions, and as he replied both of them kept looking at me so I was certain that I was the subject of their conference.

It all ended when the strange lady took me by the hand and tried to direct me inside. I resisted. It was then that my cossack became peeved; his whiskers quivered and his booming voice indicated to me in no uncertain terms that I was to go into the school. After this sudden outburst, he turned away and departed hurriedly in the direction of the railway track. It was then that the strange lady smiled at me, so realizing that valor was the better part of discretion I preceded her into the school.

I fell in love immediately. I had never ·seen so many children in one spot in my whole life, although I learned later that there were no more than ten pupils all told. I was puzzled why they sat behind one another in rows and remained so still and silent. Their positions reminded me of the many times that I had played train at home and arranged all the chairs in the house, one behind the other, just like the cars in a freight or passenger train. Maybe they played train here too. School was certainly going to be interesting if that's what they were doing. I was led to one of the empty seats, or cars as I preferred to imagine them to be, and soon became a part of the disciplined formation. Little did I realize that I would spend the next sixty years of my life in such a railroaded environment.

Not being able to communicate in the English language, I found it rather difficult to adjust to the school discipline and routine. I had to rely entirely on my powers of observation and my trial and error exploits. For instance, I didn't know I had to stay put in the desk that the teacher had first allotted to me. So when I felt tired from sitting still so long, I simply skipped over to a large desk where I could swing my legs to my heart's content. Of course the rest of the children laughed at my antics. I must have presented quite a comical sight, what with my small legs going like pistons on a steam engine, my body arched just enough to permit me to peer over the edge of the overlarge desk, and my hands clutching with all my might and main so as not to fall off. It didn't take the teacher very long to come and spoil my fun, for she took me by the hand and escorted me back to "my" desk. I also remember that after my first recess I walked in with the rest of the children and sat down in one of the big double desks at the back of the room. To me they were the "pushers," or the engines that helped the trains up the grades between the spiral tunnels in the rugged Rockies. When I looked up two boys were standing looking at me. I had taken their seat. Again the teacher came and took me by the hand, not so gently this time, and directed me to "my" desk. I was beginning to get the idea of a permanent seating plan.

I was mystified by the students who, once in a while, held up one of their hands, and when the teacher noticed them, signalled something to her by raising one, two, three, or four fingers. If she nodded approval the youngster got up and went outside, only to reappear a few minutes later seemingly much refreshed. I watched these comings and goings but couldn't see any rhyme or reason to them, so I felt that the only way I could find out was to try it myself. Up went my hand, the teacher spotted it, awkwardly I jacked up two or three of my fingers, the teacher smiled encouragingly, and I trotted outside. I felt great. I had power to do something. Now, what was I out here for? I didn't know. Certainly the other boys and girls must have gone out to do something, to get something, to receive something, or to go somewhere. I was sadly disappointed for nothing unusual happened to me, and there wasn't a thing I could see to do. So after just wandering around the school yard for a while, looking for I knew not what, I returned to the school still perplexed.

However, I solved the mystery quite unexpectedly one day when the call of nature dictated that I leave the room immediately if I was to avoid an "accident." It was then that I realized the necessity for such a unique signal system. I thought my teacher was very clever to devise the scheme.

Another thing that puzzled me was where all the white markings on the blackboard went. No magician could have baffled me more than the teacher did when I first saw her cause all the writing to vanish with one swoop of her brush. At first I assumed it had become tucked in the spaces between the colored strips of felt of the eraser and could be restored when necessary. I was wrong. A closer examination of the blackboard brush showed me it was covered with chalk dust, not writing. I then assumed that the eraser had "scrambled" the writing in much the same way my mother scrambled eggs in the frying pan. The original substance was still there but in a different form.

Whenever I was thirsty at home I merely took the dipper and helped myself to the water contained in a pail in the kitchen. At school, however, the water was kept in a handsomely decorated porcelain crock equipped with a nickel-plated push-button faucet. All I had to do was hold my cup under the faucet and push the button, and a stream of water would flow out and fill the cup. There was no mess or fuss. I thought it was ingenious and wonderful. I don't remember the number of times I went up to the front to get a drink of water the first few days, but I'm sure it was just too many. I wasn't thirsty but I enjoyed watching the water gush out of the tap. The teacher soon put an end to my experiments by placing my cup on her desk.

I also learned not to watch the other children going up for a drink or to listen to them quaffing or gulping their water. In some mysterious way the sound made me thirsty, even when I knew I wasn't. The water phenomenon soon wore off and I became one of the temperate drinkers.

Toward the end of my first day at school I dozed off. I had become tired and sleepy after such a long, exciting, and frustrating day, and the humming sound of children studying and the drone of the teacher's voice soon lulled me into a state of semiconsciousness. I was jarred back into reality almost instantly by the noise in the classroom. The children were putting away their books, rulers, pencil boxes, pens, pencils, and other paraphernalia that had accumulated on their desks. The clatter was frightening. However, as everyone seemed to be enjoying this activity, my anxiety abated. Little did I know that this uproarious interlude was the happiest time of the day for the pupils. School was over and the prospects of playing and having fun were in the offing. I soon learned that such displays of excitement and enthusiasm were a daily occurrence, at their best on a Friday or a day just before a holiday, at their lowest ebb on a Monday.

One day I was told by the teacher, and this information was repeated to me by a number of my concerned classmates, that there was to be "no school" tomorrow. I understood the meaning of the word *no* as well as the word *school* but putting the two together didn't make any sense to me. I had seen a large railway crane pick up wrecked freight cars and deposit them on flat cars with ease. But somehow I just couldn't visualize the school disappearing in any such manner. My parents were no wiser than I was about a school holiday, so the next day I took off for school as usual. I was delighted to see the school still standing in its old place. However, my joy was short-lived. Something was wrong. The door was locked and neither my teacher nor any of my classmates were around. I waited and waited, but still no one appeared.

It had become my habit to take my exercise books home every day to show and explain to my parents what I was doing in school. Their many compliments and little treats encouraged me to greater effort, and I'm sure my childish accounts and explanations provided them with some educational know-how. The younger members of the family profited from this information as well. They were receiving a school indoctrination that would prove of considerable value to them when they started school. I had lacked such conditioning and was suffering as a result. But if imitation is the sincerest form of flattery, my teacher should have been flattered many times over. I'm told I patterned all my presentations at home after her teaching mannerisms.

Since the school was closed, I kept wondering what I would show my parents that evening. I suddenly had an inspiration. I sat down on the steps of the school porch, opened my exercise book, and started to copy the words contained on a piece of paper that I found near the ash pile. I was so busy at this task that I did not notice a couple of my pals coming towards the school. Apparently they had been at our place, intent on inviting me to play with them on this holiday. However, when they were informed that I had gone to school, they immediately set out to bring me back home. Again I heard them repeat, "There's no school today, John! You can come and play ball with us. And you know what? We have a brand new ball. Come on, let's go."

I closed my books, put them under my arm, and we raced for home. All the same, I kept thinking about the strange meaning of "no school."

By the end of my first week of school, my parents decided that it would be most fitting to have a picture taken of me — just the way I looked the first day I set off for school. After all, they reasoned, their first child starting school was an important occasion in

In the era of the one-room school, there was no experience more traumatic than the day a child started school. The beginner encountered a new and confusing environment, and he left behind an empty spot at home for a few hours each day. Here is the author, John C. Charyk, in 1913 when he began school in Laggan S.D. 1063 (Lake Louise, Alberta) at five years of age.

5

their lives. So one Saturday my mother scrubbed me with a bar of Royal Crown soap until I glistened like a brand new quarter and smelled like a can of coal oil. Then she dressed me as if I were going to school but with infinitely more care than usual. When she felt I was ready for my historic picture, I accompanied my dad and two members of his section gang on a handcar to a photographer's studio in Banff, twenty-eight miles away.

There was no way they could entice me to stand alone in front of that mysterious, dark, one-eyed monster, especially with the operator hiding behind it under a black veil. As far as I was concerned, he was there for no good purpose. Eventually after a good deal of heated discussion, they indicated to me that they would stand with me. Only then did I join them.

When the photos arrived, my dad figured that the only way they could have an individual picture of me was to take a pair of scissors and snip off all the other persons. The misshapen print remained in the family album for years.

Ring the Bell and Hope for the Best

The first few days for a beginning teacher were usually filled with dismay. Nothing seemed to work, and the training received at normal school appeared remote and impractical compared to what was actually taking place in the school. No matter how much seat work was prepared, or how well it was organized, it never seemed to last for any length of time. Just the moment the teacher began taking pride in keeping a particular class busy, the students started to fool around as they completed their assignments and had nothing else to do. "I'm finished!" was the expression that was the scourge of every exasperated fledgling teacher.

Each day the thought of what the morrow might bring kept his or her mind active but full of doubt. Would he be able to keep the children gainfully occupied? Would her grade one pupils ever be able to do something on their own? Would he be able to keep order? Would the children be willing to listen and to learn? Did she honestly have enough knowledge to teach school? Would he have to work as hard and as long every evening for the rest of the year as he had done for the first few weeks? Would it be ever within reach to do the impossible and plan a timetable to give adequate time to all the classes in the eight grades?

However, as the first few weeks passed, the industrious and conscientious teacher soon realized that she was making good progress. The children were learning; the discipline, although far from perfect, was passable; the grade ones were beginning to read; and the community respected her. She also made the startling discovery that teaching was a two-way street. True, she was teaching the youngsters, but she was learning many important things from them in turn. No wonder the school boards were always looking for an experienced teacher!

Some young people seemed to be born teachers and adapted to the classroom easily and quickly; others found it difficult and had to strive hard to be successful; still others could never make a go of it. Each teacher's story is always old and yet always new. But universally, no first day of school ever turned out the way a beginning teacher had planned or hoped it would.

The normal schools certainly realized just how important such a premier day was to the future success of their graduates, so the instructors of these institutions went all out to inform these young hopefuls of how to succeed on the first day. They made it very clear that on the first morning of school, any teacher worth his salt should be in the classroom long before any of his pupils appeared on the scene; he must be there bubbling over with friendliness, enthusiasm, and zeal; and he must have the day's activities planned in careful detail.

Most new teachers tried to do as they had been taught, but unfortunately things didn't always turn out as planned. The excited pupils would begin arriving before seven o'clock in the morning. No teacher could feel and look energetic and emotive after spending a restless night in strange surroundings worrying and dreaming about first-day horrors. And who could organize for such a day when there wasn't the slightest inkling of what to organize, or for whom? Therefore, the only logical thing left for the uninitiated teacher to do was to ring the bell at the right time to get school underway and to hope for the best. Soon there would be a troop of eager and expectant youngsters ranging in age from possibly five to eighteen years parked in the desks in front of the irresolute beginner.

It was always a thrilling and anxious moment for a new teacher to look over his or her first class: thrilling because a teaching career was being launched, anxious because a feeling of inadequacy and fear assailed any beginner who realized that his or her work and influence would affect these children for good or bad for eternity. However, this wasn't the time for philosophizing, it was time for action.

Such familiar activities as repeating the Lord's Prayer, raising and saluting the flag, registering the students, and arranging the seating often provided the teacher with the necessary momentum to overcome nervousness, teach a few favorite lessons, and get the school year really underway. Somehow or other the clock would grind around to 3:30 and dismissal time. Then, when the door banged shut behind the last student as he hustled out, the silence, the peace, and the loneliness that settled on the classroom signalled the fact that the first day of teaching was over. Most teachers just sat down and enjoyed the blessed respite.

The first day of teaching is different for every teacher. No two classes, no two teachers, no two schools, no two communities are alike, so this once-in-a-lifetime experience is always unique. Here are a number of such opening-day dramas.

Glenn S. McCaughey, the son of one of the first trustees when the district was formed in 1901, recreates this scene. The students of the Concord S.D. 658 (Ponoka, Alberta) were anxiously awaiting the arrival of their new teacher. It was a chilly morning and the boys were sitting around the old box

The Stadelman children are ready for school in the Groton S.D. (Foremost, Alberta) about 1930. Note the syrup pail lunch boxes and sugar sack schoolbags.

stove speculating about what their new teacher would be like. They were also planning some tricks with which to greet the incumbent.

Unknown to the boys the subject of their conversation walked in, hung up her toque and coat, and then joined them at the stove. The students mistook her for one of the new girls. After spending a few minutes listening to the interesting plans and conjectures, she stepped to the teacher's desk, tinkled the bell, and smilingly declared, "Let's come to order now and get on with the work of the day!"

*Raising and saluting
the flag and repeating
the Lord's Prayer were
a part of the daily
opening exercises
carried out in most
Canadian rural
schools. The students of
Albermarle S.D. 2845
(Rosetown,
Saskatchewan) are just
going through their
routine one morning in
1940.*

The boys' faces turned red with humiliation. The new teacher probably weighed less than a hundred pounds, but after such a surprise introduction on the first day of school, she had no trouble, not even from the big boys.

Lucy Withnell felt that a thunderbolt which struck near the school on her first day at the Violet Dale S.D. 3499 (Czar, Alberta) was instrumental in bringing her pupils to a very close relationship with her. Pupils and teacher became a happy family right from the first day.

The first day in the first school for a young teacher just out of normal school is quite an occasion. It was for me! I was fresh from the Camrose Normal School with "big ideas" and "little know-how." It was a thrilling experience tinged with awe and fraught with plain fear. Would I do a good job? Could I handle those older boys and girls almost as big and only a few years younger than I? Strange as it may seem, a thunderbolt gave me the answer.

It was a year of terrific electrical storms. Several people had been killed by lightning, so when a storm came up on my first day of teaching at Violet Dale School, both my pupils and I were somewhat nervous. It was a particularly vicious storm, and after one blinding flash of lightning we thought our school had been struck. When the thunder had rolled away and I had calmed the children, I tried to restore their confidence. "It's all right now, something nearby has been hit, but we don't have to worry. Just settle down and rest for a few minutes. My! My! You all have such white faces."

One little lad piped up, "Teacher, your face is white too!"

We all laughed and soon were completely relaxed. I felt that from that moment on, I was accepted and respected as their teacher. We had become a family.

Not a soul was in sight that first morning of school. I was becoming more anxious by the minute wondering why somebody didn't show up. I had a forlorn feeling that maybe, just maybe, the community didn't like me and the children had been instructed to stay away from school. "That couldn't be!" I reasoned to myself. "Nobody here knows me, or has even heard of me. Oh, Lord, please send somebody!"

Then suddenly through the tears of joy welling up in my eyes, I saw a saddle horse coming over the hill, and then another, and then a democrat, and then a little girl walking, and then four or five walking together, and then a bicycle. They were a wonderful sight! I eagerly watched them, for to me they were something special. They were my first students.

I expect that on opening day the pupils went through the usual ritual of taking in every detail of my clothes, hair, shoes, and nails. Then, as they always do, they likely shifted sheepish eyes whenever I turned and looked in their direction. So long as they were attentive, I did not mind their curious stares because I thought the longer they looked the first day, the more familiar they would be on the second. I kept wondering what they thought of me and what they would say about me to one another and to their parents in the evening. One grade three boy gave me a shy smile. I interpreted it as a sign of friendliness. I was right. When the year ended, this same lad came to me and said, "You know, teacher, I didn't like school at first, but now I like it." I took his conversion as a tremendous compliment.

I'll always recall my first day in my first school because one of the trustees intro-

Going to school for the first time barefooted meant being well dressed in Keystone S.D. 3462 (Youngstown, Alberta) in the summer of 1927.

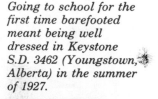

duced me to the students. What an introduction! He threatened them with the severest flogging if they misbehaved. I felt as if I was being relegated to second in command there and then. I guess the school board felt that because of my inexperience I needed some moral support. Every now and then one of the trustees would show up at the school, and although these visits didn't have anything to do with discipline, the children thought they did. Hence such business chit chats had a salutary effect. I think I played my part in this little drama rather well, for anytime a discipline problem was in the making, I reminded the potential mischiefmakers of the school board's pledge. It worked every time. However, I felt deflated when I overheard one of my senior boys whisper to his pal, "If it wasn't for the trustees she'd never make us mind!"

My opening day was beset with a problem that the instructors at the Camrose Normal School had not even mentioned, never mind suggested any way of dealing with. One pupil kept disturbing me on that first day by dashing into the school with tales of unseemly incidents taking place in the school yard. He mentioned in horrified tones that John swore; that Jim had hidden Frieda's hat in the boys' outhouse; that Keith had locked Martha in the barn; that Anna had a bag of candies but wouldn't give

any to the boys; that "they" would not give Margaret her turn at bat. Such an informer was called teacher's pet. I listened patiently to all his accusations but took no action. I must confess I just didn't know what to do under the circumstances.

Fortunately for me the bigger boys solved the problem in their own way. I learned a couple of days later that two students had rolled "my" pet in a horse blanket one recess to prevent him from reporting to me. They had also promised him similar treatments every time he blabbed. Henceforth the teacher's pet stopped squealing on his classmates.

The thing that touched me most on my first morning in the Pansy S.D. 3404 (Czar, Alberta) was the sight of the little beginners trooping to school. They accompanied their big brothers and sisters rather reluctantly, believing, no doubt, that since they were old enough to go to school they were mature enough to make their way alone. They tried to demonstrate this untested independence by carrying their own new pencil boxes and their own gaily covered scribblers. Clad in resplendent new garb, these tots made a touching picture as they trudged painfully along in shiny new shoes, swinging their dinner pails that glittered in the morning sun. Everything about them seemed to say, "We are beginners. Watch out for us!"[1]

---

1. Marjorie Dixon (teacher at Pansy S.D. 3404) in *Echoes Along the Ribstone,* Grassland Pioneers Historical Society (Provost, Alberta: Holmes Printing, 1977), 903.

Chapter Two

The Legendary One-Room Schoolhouse

Names and Numbers

The provincial ordinance relating to the formation of public school districts left the responsibility of naming each district to the local residents. It was fortuitous that the naming was left to the local authorities. Today, as a result of that policy, knowing how a school district derived its name often brings an insight into the very heart of local history and traditions. The origin of some of these school district names may be elusive, and will certainly become more elusive as time goes on, but in one way or another, many of their secrets have come to light. Our heritage is rich in such school name stories.

When a school was first contemplated for a rural district near Cayley, Alberta, in 1904, the problem of a coulee complicated matters. The homesteaders to the west wanted the school built on their side of Squaw Coulee, while those on the east were adamant that it should be on the east side. The school authorities from Regina, North-West Territories, who came out to help organize the district were unable to make much headway because of the location deadlock. Soon after, the commissioner of the Council of Public Instruction for the North-West Territories forwarded an ultimatum to the organizing school committee: the council's official would come once more, but this was the committee's "last chance." In the meantime the two factions settled their differences and decided to build the school on the bench land near the base of the west hill. What did they name their school? It just had to be the Last Chance S.D.

It was at an organizational gathering held in February 1911 at the Albert Lindquist homestead that a name was chosen for the newly formed school district near Bow Island, Alberta. A blizzard had come up during the course of the meeting, so they all stayed and enjoyed the hospitality of the Lindquist family and the comfort of a giant heater. This particular model of heater went by the captivating trade name of Good Cheer, so it didn't take them very long to make up their minds to call their school "Good Cheer" as well. It became Good Cheer S.D. 2531.

A play on words was responsible for the unique name of a school district near Lloydminster, Saskatchewan. At an organizational meeting held on May 10, 1910, an official from the Department of Education told the gathering of homesteaders the value of an education for their children and throughout the meeting kept emphasizing, "You need a school!" Apparently one potential ratepayer must have agreed with the official for he put forward a motion that the community organize a school district. The motion was passed and another enthusiastic supporter immediately shouted, "Good! Real good! Now that we have a school, let's use the name that our honorable visitor from Edmonton has been dinning into our ears all through this meeting, you need a school!" Everybody had a good laugh, but when the inventive name was brought to a vote, it was adopted almost unanimously. Thus, the Uneeda S.D. 2177 came into being.

There were so many ethnic groups in a community northeast of Lloydminster, Saskatchewan, that they could not agree on an appropriate name for their school district. The problem was that all wanted their particular origin to be reflected in the designation. No matter how hard they tried, each suggestion was turned down. Meeting after meeting ended in one stalemate after another and the situation seemed hopeless. It wasn't until Charles Despard came up with the unique title of tangled flag that the people began to voice their approval. They thought the name aptly described the ethnic makeup of not only the local district but also most early communities in the West. Agreement became unanimous when tangled flag was modified slightly to read "Tangleflags." Eventually this name became known as one of the most colorful, relevant, and interesting in the province of Saskatchewan.

There was considerable opposition to the forming of a school district near Endiang, Alberta. The residents figured it would be too hard for them to pay the necessary school taxes. At an organizational meeting held on April 25, 1912, the word "rustle" was bandied about. One indignant prospective taxpayer stated that if a school was built, the people of the district would have to rustle cattle to pay their taxes. A parent who had four children of school age and wanted a school in the worst way replied, "I agree! Sure we will have to rustle hard, but not cattle, only on our own homesteads. I read somewhere that hard work conquers all. Our children will thank us some day."

The protest of the first speaker was turned down, but his shady suggestion will be remembered for a long time. The school was named Rustle S.D. 2720.

Early settlers in the first school district at South Hill near Ogden, east of Calgary, named their school in deference to their concerns. In 1914 when the district was being organized, nearly all residents of the area were employed at the Canadian Pacific Railway Ogden shops. Feeling a close allegiance to their employer, they applied for the name CPR. However, upon learning it was illegal to use Canadian Pacific's name, they came up with a designation sounding like CPR, but spelled Cepeear S.D. 3069.

A school district founded near Central Butte, Saskatchewan, in 1912 was named Robin Hood S.D. 249. Since the livelihood of the majority of people in the district was derived from wheat farming, they thought it only fitting to name the school after the Robin Hood Flour Mills located in nearby Moose Jaw. When the trustees sought permission from the milling company to use the Robin Hood trademark, they were given a courteous "Yes." Lawrence Irving, who attended the school from 1916 to 1924, remembers rather proudly that the obliging company, recalling its rural school namesake, donated a new Union Jack for the school's flagpole on a patriotic occasion.

Some district names ran absolutely counter to the natural geographical features that characterized the area. The Violet Dale S.D. 3499 near Czar, Alberta, is a good example of such a paradox.

James Graves, a father of seven children, was one of the early homesteaders in the area, having come from the woods of Minnesota. He could neither read nor write, but

A Union Jack, a gift from the Robin Hood Flour Mills at Moose Jaw, Saskatchewan, to its namesake the Robin Hood School, waves proudly in the prairie breeze.

he was determined that his children would have "book larning." Hence it was not surprising that he became the mainspring behind the district's efforts to establish a school during the last years of World War I. The instant the new school came into being, Mr. Graves was given the honor of naming it for his new daughter, Violet. In spite of the fact that the school site was situated on the highest knoll in the surrounding flat country, he chose the name of Violet Dale.

It was the responsibility of the local people to choose a suitable name for their newly formed school district, but it was the Department of Education that assigned the number for it. In most provinces and states, there was no problem in this respect. Number one was allotted to the first school district formed, number two to the next one, and so on. However, as simple as it seemed,

it didn't turn out that way when the provinces of Alberta and Saskatchewan came into being in 1905.

When the Territorial Council set up schools in what are now Alberta and Saskatchewan, they began with Moose Jaw S.D. No. 1. From there they numbered the districts consecutively as each came into being in the North-West Territories. When the two provinces were formed, the last school enumerated by the council was Bow Valley S.D. 1409. Alberta continued to number its schools from this 1409 base; 1410, 1411, and so forth. However, Saskatchewan went back to No. 1 and filled in the numbers that had been originally assigned to the Alberta territory. Thus Saskatchewan schools are numbered consecutively from No. 1, Alberta from No. 1409 — confusing unless the system is understood.

Do It Yourself

The erection of a school in a rural district was a significant event. It meant that systematic learning was about to be introduced and that the children would be on their first step on the ladder of education. Hence it is not surprising that many of the interesting accounts surrounding the building of the local schoolhouse were recorded in the school board's minute book or in the diary or memoirs of some historically conscious early settler. Here is one such story told by William Fowlie about the Social Plains S.D. (Bindloss, Alberta).

I was only three years old when the Social Plains School was built in 1913, so I remember very little about this exciting event. But since I took all my schooling there and still live nearby, I've been concerned enough to find out some of the details from the early homesteaders.

The site selected for the schoolhouse was four miles east and eleven miles south of the present hamlet of Bindloss. At the time the

school district was formed, there was no railway in the area and Bindloss did not come into being until 1915. The closest railway town was Medicine Hat, sixty-five miles to the southeast. It could be reached by following a wagon trail that meandered through ranch leases and open country. The early settlers in the district, however, found it more expedient to use the South Saskatchewan River and raft their supplies from Medicine Hat than to go overland.

In the spring of 1913 the school board purchased the necessary lumber, bricks, and other building supplies from a lumberyard in Medicine Hat and made arrangements with two homesteaders in the district, Jack Richards and Richard Stowe, to construct a raft of this material and float it down the South Saskatchewan River to a place called Tucker's Landing. From there the supplies were hauled by horse and wagon to the school site, six miles away.

The task of building the school became a community effort. John Antiumpti, a homesteader who was also a skilled carpenter, was put in charge of building the school, with other volunteers in the district taking their turns as helpers. Since John's homestead was on the quarter section adjoining the school site on the north, it was possible for him to oversee the construction of the schoolhouse at all times.

The building was finished on the outside with cedar siding and on the inside with lath and plaster. This plastering work was done by Wesley Vaughn, who had been a mason prior to taking up his homestead in the district. He also built the chimney. However, contrary to local practice, Wesley built it from the ground up, and its top towered dizzily several feet above the hiproof of the school.

In fact, while he was still in the process of erecting it, a number of apprehensive residents of the district suggested he support it with braces to make it safe. Whereupon Mr. Vaughn, being a quick-tempered individual, informed his advisors in no uncertain manner that if they thought he could not build a chimney that would stand up, they could build their own chimney. The school board quickly came to his support and persuaded him to continue his work on the chimney in

A classic picture of the one-room rural school was one showing the children at play during the noon hour or recess. This one is of the students of Westover S.D. 2754 (Richdale, Alberta) playing "scrub" in the schoolyard. The barbed-wire fence in the foreground and the teacherage and outhouse in the background are the only other breaks in the stark and barren landscape.

his own way and not listen to the sidewalk superintendents.

Today, seventy years later, the chimney remains straight and tall, just like the day he built it. In fact, the original school stands on its initial site, as sturdy as when it was first erected. It has always received excellent care from the district residents. A number of these people went to school there, one taught there for a number of years, and those who moved into the area

No educational frills in this Angusville classroom (Angusville, Manitoba) in about 1920. The interior, the furnishings, and the equipment in many rural schools could best be described as containing only the "bare" essentials.

15

during the intervening years all consider the Social Plains School a part of their heritage. It is something to be revered and preserved. They proudly say, "It's ours! We built it and we'll always look after it!"

The farmer-carpenters who built the school for the Figure Eight Lake S.D. 4475 (Berwyn, Alberta) in 1931 misinterpreted

Catching fire was a tragedy that beset many rural schools. Mae (Lienhart) Alexander, a teacher, remembers what happened to her school in Georgetown S.D. 3232 (Delia, Alberta) in 1925. "As I returned to the district after spending a few days at my home in Calgary, I was told that there had been a fire in my school and it would be closed for a month."

the blueprints and fastened the door to swing inwards. As a result, after every heavy rain the door stuck so tightly that on one occasion the combined strength of the pupils and teacher failed to budge it. On another occasion the pupils and teacher were still shut in at five o'clock. It wasn't until a father became anxious about the late return of his son and went to the school to investigate that they were freed. The door

was changed soon after this embarrassing incident.

This is not an isolated example of a blunder made in constructing a rural school. The early schools were planned and built by people who were not professional carpenters or builders, so mistakes were quite common, even where blueprints were supplied. In fact, some of the bunglings stemmed from the fact that these self-styled contractors had difficulties in interpreting blueprints correctly. Hence more than one school ended up with all its windows on the wrong side, or the pitch of the roof too steep, or the chimney located at the wrong end of the school, or the blackboards too high for the smaller pupils to reach, or a ceiling that was too high or too low, or an inadequate ventilating system. Unfortunately, most of these mistakes were not detected for months and by that time it was too late to do anything about them. It was the students and teacher who suffered most from these construction miscues.

Without a doubt, faulty illumination was the worst offender. It has been estimated from a survey of inspectors' reports that well over fifty percent of early rural schools had improper or inadequate lighting. Most deficiencies stemmed from improper placement of the windows. The official regulation that "the total area of window glass must be

The school barn in Kirkwald S.D. 2463 (Oyen, Alberta).

equal to at least one-fifth of the floor space" was observed only superficially. Contractors reasoned that as long as the school was built with enough window space it would be adequately lighted, regardless of where the windows were placed. Originally, many schools were constructed with windows on both sides; others had them installed on three sides. It took years to convince local school boards of the harmful effects of cross

lighting, never mind such incidentals as pupils consistently having to face a window or windows from their assigned locations in the classroom; the lack of the required minimum standard of luminosity on each desk and on the blackboard; or the rule that most of the light should come from windows on the pupils' left. In the meantime the unfortunate students squinted from too much light, from cross lighting, or from

The interior of a school railway car, showing a geography lesson in progress. The cars were used in northern Ontario in the 1930s to provide schooling for children living in isolated parts of the province not yet served by rural districts.

17

always having to write in their own shadow. To make matters worse, very few schools were equipped with coal oil lamps or other forms of artificial lighting that could be used to supplement the inadequate natural light on overcast days or during a black blizzard. These lighting problems continued to haunt the students and their teachers for years to come because for many districts correcting them would have meant rebuilding some parts of their schools, which they could ill afford.

No matter how these one-room schoolhouses were built, to the youngsters who attended them, they seemed inordinately large. Yet visiting them years later, they appeared to be impossibly small. As Walter Siewert of the Janet S.D. 3609 (Chestermere Lake, Alberta) so aptly observed, "I'd swear the darn thing shrunk!"

The District Timepiece

Very few rural schools possessed the so-called school clock which is proving so popular today as a prized antique. It seemed much too extravagant for a newly formed school district to order a clock in its first requisition for supplies. Desks, maps, blackboard brushes, chalk, a globe, a dictionary, a water fountain, a washbasin, and the like were understandable, but a clock! Yet some school boards spent six dollars of their limited funds to obtain such an apparent educational nonentity.

The main purpose of the purchase was to provide a master timekeeper for the district. It must be understood that during the early days very few households owned more than one timepiece, and district residents were always confronted with the problem, "What is the correct time?" A clock in the schoolhouse was the answer. Eventually, everyone was operating by the "school time," sometimes flippantly referred to as the "teacher's time."

The all-important clock was usually an octagonal or hexagonal wall model with an oak or walnut finish, an eight-day movement, a visible pendulum, and a ten- to twelve-inch dial with Roman numerals. It hung for years at the front of the room, sometimes ticktocking merrily, at other times remaining as silent as the tombs; sometimes showing the correct time but just as frequently way off the mark.

The whim of the teacher, and occasionally of the pupils, had much to do with the performance or the lack of performance of the clock. If they wound it regularly, kept it set correctly, and did not fool around with it, the clock faithfully fulfilled its intended role. In fact its pleasant ticktock became a welcome refrain during the times the children needed a little comforting — staying in after school or writing the final departmental examinations.

Most students believed that their school clock was about the slowest-running timepiece in existence. All morning long the youngsters thought the leisurely hands would never point to twelve o'clock and all the exciting noon hour activities they were anticipating. In the afternoon, if anything, the hands took even longer to reach the magical hour of 3:30. And if a child was unfortunate enough to have to stay in after school, that clock on the wall just seemed to have stopped altogether. There was no way a pupil could trust that fickle white face. During class time the pendulum swung oh, so lazily, but when recess or the lunch hour arrived with interesting things to do, the stupid thing would speed up. Only a school clock would ever take advantage of children in such a rash manner while they were outside for a little fun and not able to watch the time. No doubt about it: The clock was in league with the teacher!

A seventy-year-old school clock still points to the hour that was most popular with students throughout the history of the one-room rural school.

Oh, for a Drink of Water

One of the most frustrating problems that confronted the majority of early rural schools was how to provide an adequate supply of good drinking water when there didn't seem to be any nearby. Digging a well on the school grounds never assured the school board that water would be found, or, if found, usable. Sometimes the water discovered had a peculiar taste, was off-color,

The rural teacher's domain: the schoolhouse, coal shed, and water pump of Rush Centre S.D. 2769 (Oyen, Alberta) in 1943.

had purgative properties, was contaminated in some way, or possessed other adverse characteristics. The inconvenient alternative was to hire someone to bring a daily supply from a neighboring well, river, lake, spring, or creek; or better still have the pupils bring their own supply from home. The latter scheme was the option chosen by most school districts in their formative years. At least this method was simple, didn't cost the school board any money, and functioned without any kind of direction.

The trustees may have preferred this scheme, but the students didn't. It was difficult for those who walked or rode horseback to tote such an unhandy substance as water. So students resorted to using unique containers in which to carry their drinking water to school: baby milk bottles, long-snouted oiling cans, hip flasks, demijohns, canvas bags, jugs of all types,

and even hot-water bottles. Anything that could hold water and prevent spillage under jolting, was convenient to handle and cart, was quickly adopted by the sharp-witted youngsters. Unfortunately, the amount of liquid that could be carried in such receptacles was limited and usually disappeared long before the end of the school day. As a consequence some children had to go thirsty, and how could they give their best performance in the classroom under such circumstances. Besides, by late afternoon on a hot summer day, whatever had been saved by a frugal child would have become tepid and almost useless.

Is it any wonder then, that the seemingly simple problem of providing a daily supply of drinking water in the rural schools spawned so many human interest stories? Here is one such account from the Aylesford S.D. 2836 (Maple Creek, Saskatchewan) as told by Peter Perrin, a former pupil of the school.

There was no drinking water at the school so the pupils were instructed to bring their own. Occasionally some of the youngsters forgot to bring their supply, or felt they could do without for that day. If it happened to turn warm, those now very thirsty and unhappy souls would decide to run to the west and fill a Roger's syrup pail or a bottle from Hay Creek. Since the stream was murky near the school, water had to be taken from places farther downstream where the water had become lukewarm. Cow Creek to the east was closer, but smaller, so the water was even warmer. On hot days the cows would stand in the creek farther up, to protect themselves from the flies. It didn't take a very smart grade one pupil to know from the taste of the water why it was called Cow Creek. There was little likelihood of anyone calling it "taster's choice." It was years before our school board decided to provide us with a water dispenser in the form of a pail and a dipper and to hire someone to bring a fresh supply of drinking water to school every day. Then we had to wait another few years before a proper water crock made its appearance.

Although the Skipton S.D. (Leask, Saskatchewan) didn't experience any difficulty in obtaining an ample supply of good drinking water from a well right on the school premises, the teacher's attempts to introduce a sanitary method of drinking it weren't too successful. Alice Webb, who attended the school in the early days, recalls the problem rather vividly.

Our liquid refreshments came from the well — delicious, ice cold water, or "Adam's ale," as we preferred to call it. Someone would haul up a pail by means of the rope and pulley, and we would all have our turn drinking out of the large, blue-enameled mug. At least I think it was blue. It was so well covered with rust it was hard to really know. Every spring when we started back to school, some of us arrived with our own drinking cups. These eventually disappeared or were broken early in the term, but that was a mere detail. It was much handier just to use the old mug which was always

The drinking and washing facilities in most early one-room schools, like this one in Leader S.D. 3372 (Leader, Saskatchewan) in 1948, consisted of a small bench, a cream can of drinking water, a common drinking cup, a washbasin, a bar of soap, a wash rag, a towel, and a slop bucket. A corner storage cupboard was reserved for the lunch pails and homework aids like textbooks, reference readers, and exercise books.

there. I don't remember any of us having to stay home from school because of an outbreak of measles, chickenpox, or any of the other communicable diseases common to childhood.

Drinking water for the school and teacherage in the Aurora S.D. 1050 (Winnipeg, Manitoba) was obtained from a well some fifty feet away. It was cold and pure and received regular government inspection to keep it that way. However, there was one period during which it may have fallen below the required standards. The thirties were known not only for dust and drought but also for the tremendous increase in the grasshopper population. Somehow, despite all attempts to get rid of them, the pesky creatures kept falling into the school well. The pioneer spirit that had settled the land couldn't all have disappeared by that time, for some brave soul decided that a few "hoppers" in the drinking water weren't a hopeless problem. Consequently, one day the children found a small white cotton bag draped neatly around the spout of the pump. The purpose of the bag was to filter out the extraneous things in the water. It proved to be most successful, and the water emerging from the spout and through the cotton bag was free of grasshoppers. Anytime the bag became a bit bulky, it was removed and the sodden mass of drowned grasshoppers and other squashy-looking fauna was dumped to one side. Strangely enough, the procedure didn't bother the youngsters at all.

Getting a pail of water was never simple

Getting a pail of water was an experience that very few rural students ever forgot. A pail was the method and two pupils were the means. There was no set pattern for carrying the water. Any youngster not lucky enough to escape the teacher's eye at the time the fountain, crock, or pail became empty was delegated to take a classmate with him and bring back a pail of water. The buddy system was, no doubt, insurance against the first pupil falling into the well,

the creek, or the lake, and not having anyone to report the matter. Usually the teacher had no difficulty in obtaining volunteers when the weather was fine, for the task meant a welcome escape from the humdrum routine of the classroom. But in wintertime, only the intrepid were equal to the trip.

On the way to the source of water, there were gophers and field mice to stalk, stones to throw, birds to tease, and an opportunity to bask in the sunshine and enjoy nature. However, the return trip meant work, hard work. It wasn't easy to carry a pail full of water that weighed in the neighborhood of fifty pounds a distance of a quarter of a mile or more. Any jostling, no matter how minimal, had the effect of impelling the water to slosh around in the pail and eventually to splash over the rim. Swerving water is difficult to carry, so unless the porters acted in concert in all their movements, especially their gait, the water splashed on them, soaked their clothes, trickled down their legs into their shoes, and made them feel miserable. Often the youngsters exchanged sides to rest their tired and benumbed hands and arms.

No matter how hard the carriers tried to keep the water in prime condition, by the time they reached the school there was always something wrong with it. If they walked back leisurely on a pleasant summer day, the water would be warm. But if they hurried, most of it spilled out. And no matter whether they took their time or rushed, blades of grass, specks of dirt, a fly or two, a few grass fleas, a spider, and maybe a grasshopper inevitably appeared floating on the water. Nevertheless, in spite of these impurities, the students whose thirst had been growing by the minute since the departure of the water fetchers quaffed the fresh cold water with a gusto that rewarded the two volunteers for their trouble.

Conditions for carrying water were a little more favorable in the wintertime. The probability of impurities falling into the water was reduced considerably. Then again, as the students' concerns had switched from quenching their thirst to keeping warm, the need for water was reduced. As a consequence, fewer trips had to be made to the well or the spring or the river. However, winter brought its own unique problems for both the teacher and the couriers, as the incident described below indicates.

One late autumn afternoon in 1894 in the Union Point S.D. 53 (Ste. Agathe, Manitoba), it started to snow heavily. In a short time the ground was covered with a two-inch blanket. Two boys, undaunted by the sudden change in the weather, volunteered to venture into the cold whiteness and bring back a pail of fresh water from the school's usual source of drinking water, the Red River a quarter of a mile away. Once on their way, they discovered much to their chagrin that it was much colder than they had expected. So instead of loitering along the way back as they had planned, they made up their minds to run with their liquid cargo. Their strategy didn't work too well, for they spilled most of the water. In fact, they had almost decided to return to the river for a refill when one of them came up with a brilliant idea. Why not make up the loss by substituting snow? They reasoned that it would melt and no one would notice the difference. All water looked alike whether it came from the river or from the melted snow. Unfortunately, much to their surprise the snow failed to liquefy. It merely mixed with the water and formed slush.

The two schemers reached the school just in time for recess. One look at the snowy concoction and the surprised teacher shook her head and tersely said, "I didn't think it was snowing that hard! Thanks just the same, boys."

Once the pail was set in its usual place on the unused desk at the back of the room, a number of thirsty pupils gathered around, stared at the snowy mixture, and quickly changed their minds about taking a drink. Not many minutes passed before a grade seven girl devised a use for the snowy sop. She secretly snatched up a handful and slipped the watery snowball down the back of the shirt of one of the water carriers. The results were instantaneous. The lad gasped, shivered, let out a cry, and started to prance

The students from Aylesford S.D. 2838 (Maple Creek, Saskatchewan) at times drank water from Cow Creek, shown here.

around in an attempt to dislodge the icy passenger. His torment appeared to be the signal for a number of other children to grab handfuls of the melting snow and pelt the two fakers, and anybody else who came into their range. Within minutes the classroom floor was so spattered with snow and water that the teacher quickly tapped her desk bell and brought an end to the recess, and to the slushy fray.

A number of rural schools solved their drinking water problem by melting ice. One such school was the Figure Eight Lake S.D. 4475 (Berwyn, Alberta). A special shed was constructed on the school premises, and during the early spring the trustees hired someone to haul ice from a nearby lake or river. The blocks were stored in this ice-house in sawdust or a similar insulating material. Whenever drinking water was required, a chunk or two of ice would be brought into the school and deposited in the crock or water pail, and the warmth of the room did the rest.

Now and then the school would experience some difficulty in removing all the sawdust particles from the block of ice, or even of having the ice melt. The latter was a real problem on cool days and was usually solved by stoking up the stove so more heat would be produced. Any particles of dust that found their way into the drinking water were easily removed by pouring the water through an ordinary milk strainer that was kept handy on a nearby peg.

The amount of drinking water that the students needed for a particular day and the temperature required to melt enough ice to insure the supply should have performed in close harmony. On hot days when everybody was thirsty, the ice would melt quickly and there would be plenty of water for all; on a cold day when very few pupils needed a drink, the ice would melt slowly and the water supply would be reduced accordingly. Theoretically this idea should have worked, but in actual practice, as far as the students were concerned, the ice melted all too slowly and there was always a shortage of water. Hence it was a common sight to see a youngster sucking away on a piece of ice to quench his thirst rather than waiting for the ice to melt in the pail or crock. However, there was one consolation for those who had the patience to wait: The water was always ice cold and it didn't take much to satiate their thirst.

During wintertime solution of the drinking water problem was simple. The students turned to eating the snow or the icicles that they found on the roof of the barn or the school porch. Besides, as long as suitable ice was available outside, the process of melting continued.

This ice-melting method of providing drinking water had its disadvantages. In a number of instances the workmen who packed the ice in sawdust were inexperienced or inept, and the ice melted while still in the icehouse. Occasionally, unscrupulous individuals helped themselves to the ice stored in the school icehouse for making ice cream or for other such domestic purposes. Again the students were the ultimate losers. Unless the icehouse was closely supervised it had the potential of becoming a den for all types of misbehavior. Former students when reminiscing about the icehouse often referred to it as the "smoke house," probably with good reason.

Most of the youngsters hated it. There were no fond memories here. Digging out a block of ice from its tomb in the sawdust, washing it, breaking it into manageable pieces, and then carrying them into the schoolhouse was a very messy and arduous task. Few pupils enjoyed doing this chore when their turn came around.

Cleaning the school well

Good drinking water was so important to the pupils of any rural school that they were willing to make sacrifices and help in any way they could to get an ample supply and to see that it was free from impurities and had a good taste. The children in the Youngville S.D. 3621 (Athabasca, Alberta) were more instrumental than most in trying to improve the quality of their drinking water.

There was no well when the school was first built in 1917 so the pupils were responsible for bringing their own supply of drinking water. Four years later after a well had been dug, the cribbing installed, and a cover built over the top, the school board members felt that they had made short work of their water problem.

Resolution wasn't that easy. A peek down the well always revealed a dead mouse, gopher, rabbit, or insects of one type or another floating around in the water. Every so often when someone caught sight of such decaying objects, the water was declared unfit to drink; otherwise, no one was any wiser and continued to drink the water.

One day when the bigger boys discovered a dead gopher in the water, they quickly made up their minds to give the well a good cleanup once and for all. The water was bailed out and a lad volunteered to crawl down and remove the decaying animal. It didn't take him very long to gather all the remains and deposit them in the bucket that had been lowered into the well. Soon he gave the signal, and the boy at the windlass proceeded to draw up the pail. Unfortunately, when he had raised it halfway up, the school bell rang. In his excitement to race to the school and beat the other boys, he let go of the rope. Down dropped the mud, the dead animal and decaying vegetation, right on top of the faithful lad at the bottom of the well. Although he was almost knocked unconscious and received a deep gash on the side of his head, nothing more serious happened. It was only after the teacher started to make inquiries about the whereabouts of her grade eight pupil that she learned he was still down the well.

The Waterman-Waterbury Heater

Of the various models of heaters used in the one-room rural school, the one manufactured by the Waterman-Waterbury Company of Minneapolis, Minnesota, was the best known. No matter what type of pot-bellied stove the school purchased when it first started operating, most eventually changed over to the Waterman-Waterbury product. In fact, the history of the rural school and that of the Waterman-Waterbury heater were so intimately related that one seldom heard mention of one without the other.

The installation of this make of stove followed a set pattern. It was placed in one of the corners at the back of the room and then connected to a brick chimney at the opposite end with a prodigious length of overhead eight-inch stovepipes. Part of the accepted technique for heating schools in the early days was the theory that the longer the line of pipes that meandered aloft, the more heat was bound to radiate from their combined surfaces.

The real success of the Waterman-Waterbury heater stemmed from its gargantuan size, which provided a vast heating surface, and from the five-foot-high, double-layered, insulated sheet metal jacket that enclosed it like a huge cylinder. The sides and back of the jacket were supported by steel struts, while the front quarter was mounted on hinges and could be swung open or closed like a door or gate. Since the architects knew that this particular model was destined for schools, they did their part for art education by embossing the entire surface of the metal jacket with intriguing circular designs. Their parting gesture was to garb the whole thing in glossy black.

It didn't require an expert to fathom the mystery of how this monster heater worked. The cold air was drawn from the floor at the bottom of the stove. Confined by the jacket, it circulated around the hot surface of the heater until it became warm and rose upwards towards the ceiling. At the same time the cold air in the classroom descended and once more moved along the floor towards the foot of the stove to start repeating the heating process. The air circulated so rapidly and positively that the room became free from any cold corners. The temperature varied only three or four degrees between the floor and the ceiling.

In addition, there was a duct that connected the fresh air vent on the outside of the schoolhouse to a point just behind the stove to provide a continuous supply of fresh air. Unfortunately, in most schools the duct turned out to be a cold air intake and nothing more. No one, least of all the pupils and their teacher, wanted more cold air in the classroom, a place that was already too cold for comfort.

Over the years their complaint that the school was cold couldn't be understood. How could anything as scientific, as modern, and as expensive ($168 in 1923) as the Waterbury furnace not work perfectly? However, sooner or later some local genius would resolve the problem by simply plugging the outside duct. Not infrequently, children at play or even merciful Nature

*The
Waterman-Waterbury
stove, "scientific,
modern, and expensive"
(at $168 in 1923).*

with her blizzards and dust storms would accomplish the same result without any fanfare. Once the outside air could no longer flow into the school through the duct, the air already in the building kept circulating, becoming warmer with each pass through the jacket. The children were not even deprived of fresh air, as enough entered the classroom through the cracks around the ill-fitting door and the single-glazed windows or filtered through the thin floor.

Mrs. Allen Bateman of the Big Bend S.D. 809 (Innisfail, Alberta) describes one of the procedures used in 1903.

Many a wintry morning the first item on the day's agenda was a brisk march around the desks. This activity not only warmed numbed toes and fingers but also tended to circulate the air so at least some heat from the faithful potbellied stove found its way to every corner.

There were a number of contrivances on the Waterman-Waterbury heater that could be manipulated singly or in various combinations to operate it successfully: the ash-pit door and its slide-draft regulator, the fuel-feed door and its particular style of slide-draft controller, the duplex dumping grate, the grate shaker, and the stovepipe damper. When all the variables of operation are considered, is it any wonder that the person who tended the Waterman-Waterbury stove referred to it as a temperamental steel robot — fickle as a woman, stubborn as a mule, but sensitive to even the smallest act of attention and respect.

The Waterman-Waterbury Manufacturing Company, which established its Canadian West headquarters in Regina, Saskatchewan, was very innovative in its methods of promoting the school stoves. George Fitch, whose father was chairman of the first school board formed in the Centerville S.D. 791 (Red Deer, Alberta) in 1903, describes one such memorable event that took place in the district in 1912.

A Mr. Babcock, who represented the Waterman-Waterbury Manufacturing Company, held a public meeting in the school.

The residents were out in full force to hear his lecture on air and heating systems and to enjoy his many songs accompanied by Miss A. G. Crowe, an accomplished musician and the Centerville teacher at the time. Needless to say, all favored the new heating setup, which was installed during Christmas week. This furnace gave many years of satisfactory service.

All rural teachers, at one time or another, had to struggle with the eccentricities of the school heater. It took all their ingenuity to start, stoke, adjust drafts, and bank it, so their students could study and learn in comparative comfort. During the years when the depression deepened, the summers became drier, and the winters harder, the problem of obtaining coal, wood, and even paper to light the fire became crucial. Frank Jacobs of the McCann S.D. 2562 (Stanmore, Alberta) describes how difficult it was to obtain paper to light the school fire in the thirties.

One of the older boys in the school lit the fire in the Waterman-Waterbury furnace every morning. He used straw to light the fires. Yes, straw! Practically no one in the district had enough newspapers, magazines, or any other mail to light the fires at home and have any left over to light the school stove too. And unfortunately, the straw that lit the school fire could have been used for feed for the half-starved work horses and the milk cow.

In spite of the special care and attention that most school stoves received, accidents still happened. Take the supposedly simple matter of banking the fire overnight so it could be quickly restarted in the morning. All it involved was covering the glowing embers with a fresh supply of coal and adjusting the drafts to keep the fire inactive. Yet strange things happened.

During the winter of 1930 the North Star S.D. 577 (Clive, Alberta) was nearly destroyed by fire because the student-fireman was not familiar with the proper way of banking the stove. One of the older boys

School children and firewood really got to know each other intimately during a cold winter in the thirties in Hazeldean S.D. 195 (Deloraine, Manitoba).

who was acting as janitor banked the old Waterman-Waterbury heater with large lumps of coal for the night. One of the lumps fell against the door and pushed it open, and hot coals spilled out over the floor. When the regular caretaker arrived early the next morning, he discovered a good-sized hole burnt through the floor. By some miracle the wooden planks had not actually caught fire, only charred.

Local school officials were always on the lookout for ways to improve the efficiency of their heaters. So it wasn't long before a number of schools removed either the complete stove jacket or just the door section. Two reasons were given for doing the latter. First, the students arriving at school on a bitterly cold morning with frost-bitten toes, fingers, and faces were never able to secure immediate relief because of the metal screen between them and the hot stove. Secondly, the strident clatter and thump of the tin door every time it was opened or closed was disturbing and nerve-racking to the pupils studying or reciting.

The majority of rural schoolhouses were simple frame structures, well known for their cold and drafty conditions, especially during winter. The following incident is related by Mrs. Jean Black, a 1945 student in the Fairfield S.D. (Coronation, Alberta). It reveals not only the hardships of trying to study under conditions of intense cold but also the embarrassing possibilities of the ever-present potbellied stove.

It was a cold, snowy morning as my sister and I, riding double on Maud, made our way towards the Fairfield schoolhouse. A northwest wind made matters worse and before long my fingers became numb as the frost bit through my mittens. Sis, clinging to my back, was whimpering because she was getting colder by the minute. I kept urging Maud to go a little faster, but she stubbornly refused to change her pace. Slow and steady was good enough for her, so slow and steady had to be good enough for us. With a sigh of relief we finally caught sight of the school through the swirling snow.

I stopped Maud at the school steps, let Sis off, and then continued down to the barn. The warm, pungent smell of horses greeted me as I opened the door. I felt like staying there to absorb some of the welcome heat, but it was almost time for school to start. I quickly unsaddled the horse, tied her up in her stall, and raced for the school. The instant I opened the school door, a blast of frigid air greeted me. It was nearly as cold inside the cloakroom as it was outside, so I left my coat on. When I entered the classroom, the teacher was bent over the stove trying to get the stubborn fire going while my classmates huddled around trying to warm themselves as best as they could.

The room was still cold when it came time to call school, so the teacher permitted us to remain around the stove while we repeated the Lord's Prayer and saluted the flag. He then read to us for over a quarter of an hour.

When we finally did return to our regular desks, it was hard to concentrate on what the teacher was telling us. Our minds couldn't absorb very much while our bodies were so cold. Several times the teacher had to call my name twice before I realized he was speaking to me. The other children were shivering, squirming around in their desks, tapping their feet, blowing into their cupped hands, or rubbing them vigorously together. It all seemed like an exercise in futility, for as long as the stove failed to provide any heat, we remained chilly and uncomfortable.

Finally, the long awaited command, "Okay, it's time for lunch!" was given. Immediately books were slammed shut and stuffed into desks and a general exodus began as the students dashed out to the cloakroom to pick up their lunch pails or to the barn to feed the horses. The stove also responded to this noon hour freedom. It gave out some much appreciated heat.

I received a pleasant surprise when I opened my lunch pail, a can of beans. I guess my mother had wanted to give me something extra on such a cold day. Since the beans were frozen solid, I set the can on top of the now resurgent stove and went back to my desk to do some work. Five minutes later when I returned to pick up my can of beans, I found it so hot that I nearly dropped it and just managed to carry it to the nearest desk — the teacher's. After waiting a minute or two, I decided it was cool enough to open so as usual I punched a hole in the lid with my knife. I wasn't prepared for the explosion that resulted. Beans shot everywhere! They struck me, the ceiling, a window, the nearby desks, and even a map on the wall.

Our teacher had gone out to the cloakroom, but when he heard all the commotion he hurried back to see what was going on. He stopped in the doorway as if petrified and stared at the mess. Then his eyes fell on the bean-smeared map. From the piqued expression on his face, I thought for a moment he was going to hit me, or do something even more vicious. However, after his initial shock, he composed himself and even gave me a wry smile. He went to his desk, pulled out a cloth, handed it to me, and told me to get to work immediately and clean up the mess.

I was able to scrub the beans off everything except the all-important map. No matter how hard I tried, the brown stains remained. It happened to be a map that showed where different crops were grown in Canada. From then on the children jokingly referred to the brown spots as the areas where beans were grown.

That evening I told my mom that the bean explosion was the most embarrassing experience I had ever had. I also told her that I never wanted to see another can of beans, no matter how cold it got.

Today, I smile to myself every time I recall the "bean volcano," but at the same time I can't help but sympathize with my teacher. It must have been a very exasperating scene to come upon.

Outhouse Blues

The privy or outhouse was well named, for it was an ingenious device for preserving human privacy. It was the source of ribald humor as people in those arduous times made light of trying situations.

Most rural students will never forget the jaunt to the school outhouse that could not be forestalled, even on a winter day after the winds had piled the snow over the very throne of the airy building. The experience of sweeping or shovelling the snow from the seat and then receiving its chilly and nipping reception in below zero weather wasn't very pleasant. Indeed, the torture of the icy seat was enough to make a Spartan sob.

Duties were performed with dispatch, as it was not a place where one cared to linger. The youngsters wore so many clothes in those days that it was like taking part in an arctic expedition to go to the outdoor toilet. To make matters worse, zippers had not as yet been invented, and to fumble with a multitude of buttons and buttonholes with cold, numb fingers was a formidable task.

It seems strange that very little was done to provide some conveniences for the pupils who had to go to the outhouse on a cold day. The Prestville S.D. (Spirit River, Alberta) was the rare exception.

When J. B. Strain, the present superintendent of schools for the town of Stettler, first taught in the Prestville School, he was surprised to discover an ingenious home-made toilet seat hanging on the wall of the classroom, just out of sight behind the heater. At first he surmised it was some kind of a joke, but he later changed his mind when the cold, snowy weather arrived and he discovered how practical and well intentioned such an appliance turned out to be. Any student who had a need to go to the outhouse put on his outdoor clothes, removed the seat from its peg on the wall without any embarrassment or conceit, and shuffled outdoors. It doesn't take much imagination to realize how useful and convenient such a portable toilet seat could be. When the youngster returned to the classroom, he would also bring back the all-important seat and hang it in its accustomed place, ready for the next user.

It's strange that such a simple and expedient method of overcoming the discomfort of the icy, snow-covered toilet seat of an outdoor biffy wasn't adopted by more rural schools. Apparently, accepting things the way they were was a sure way to stop progress, even with outhouse facilities.

Locked in

Today no one can be locked in a school or any other public building. Mechanical devices such as panic bars and the general rule that doors must open outwards have taken care of such accidents. However, in the days of the one-room schoolhouse, there were few safeguards, so occasionally students found themselves locked in the schoolhouse, the barn, the coal shed, or the outhouse. The outhouse in particular was the site for many of the lock-ins. The doors of the early models of these conveniences opened outwards, and the outside latch was a wooden spindle.

Mrs. G. Hedberg relates her experience in the Blaeberry S.D. (Golden, British Columbia) in 1933, revealing what it feels like to be the victim of an outhouse lock-in.

We had occasional outhouse trouble in our school. The real cause was the outside latch, which was nothing more than a piece of wood with a nail driven through the middle. One day the bell rang while I was in there, and when I tried the door it was locked. I pushed it, shook it, booted it, flung my body against it, and even tried to batter it down with my fists. It didn't budge. I was trapped like a wild animal in a cage, and I felt just like one — helpless, miserable, and forlorn. Strange thoughts began to swirl through my brain. What if everybody went home and left me here for the night? It could happen! Why haven't they missed me in the school? They should have by now. Surely the teacher can see that my desk is empty and realize that something is wrong. Woe is me! I guess they don't care about me. Oh, well, I'm sure my parents will come looking for me when school is over and I don't get home at my accustomed time.

Then suddenly I had a bright idea. There was a girl in the school that I detested, and I felt sure she had locked me in. Now I knew what to do! I began to holler as loudly as I could, "I'm in the toilet! Florence locked me in! I'm in the toilet! Florence locked me in!" I was almost yelling in singsong fashion. I would have loved to get Florence into trouble, and now was my chance.

I kept shouting at the top of my voice until someone heard me and let me out. The teacher didn't punish Florence in spite of my many accusations. In fact, a few days later Florence herself got locked in there. I'm certain she thought I had done it, but I wasn't responsible. Both times the wind had spun the rotary latch around until it had locked the door from the outside.

The missing toilet paper

In these days of high pressure advertising of bathroom tissue, it is difficult to believe that not so long ago, the only toilet "tissues" available in the rural school outhouses consisted of old issues of Eaton's catalogues, outdated newspapers and magazines, and (in the appropriate seasons) a handful of grass, a corn cob, or broad leaves. Students never dared waste the apple tissue papers in which their jam sandwiches were usually wrapped. In fact, at Christmas time it was considered a special treat to have the flimsy wrappings from oranges and apples instead of the rough pages from the catalogues and newspapers or the slithery rotogravure sheets that usually littered the outhouse.

Today, students would greet with scepticism any hearsay that rural students used to

The two outhouses in Merrickville S.D. 4114 (Sibbald, Alberta) in 1943 afforded a view for miles in any direction.

hide apple or orange tissue papers in their desks, carry them around in their pockets, fold them inside their readers, and at times even use them as a medium of exchange. The best scroungers in the school had a secret cache of such needed and luxurious toilet tissues and were ready to peddle them for a price. In Cherry Valley S.D. 3087 (Oyen, Alberta) the barter rate right after Christmas in 1930 was as follows: two orange wrappings were worth a piece of candy, a sandwich, two cookies, or a piece of cake; one orange wrapping enabled a student to borrow an eraser, a pen, a paint brush, a compass, or a ruler; three tissues (in good shape) qualified a student for help with his homework, a ride home in a buggy, or relief from the chore of lighting the school heater on a particular morning. It must be realized that the children in those days, just like the adults, made light of things that were trying. So it is not surprising to find that an inelegant necessity like toilet paper was the source of earthy humor.

Facing page

A much-prized receipt for gopher tails. During years of severe gopher infestations, rural municipalities on the prairies paid a bounty of about one cent for each gopher tail turned in. The school children in the Sunnynook area of Alberta found the gopher-tail venture a rather rewarding one in 1932.

Shirley Marlowe, then the teacher at the Greenmound School, supplies the following story.

The moment the trustees of the Greenmound S.D. 2734 (Oyen, Alberta) decided to introduce "real" toilet paper into the school's two outhouses, the district residents felt that education had really "gone modern."

Thumbing through the latest edition of the Western School Supply Company catalogue, school board members happened to glance at the price of toilet paper: "Five cents per roll, or a case of one hundred rolls at four dollars and fifty cents." They all agreed that the price was right and before long had convinced one another that it would be a good idea to order some for the school's two outhouses. The question of how many rolls would be required of course came up. Being down-to-earth individuals, they proceeded to do some calculations.

"Let's see now. Two sheets per student per schoolday ... that would come to.... It's not going to work! Some students might get sick, and then again those kids might use it for other things. Let's say three sheets per student per school day. We've forgotten the teacher! And what's going to happen when we have our dances and parties at the schoolhouse?"

In the end the board members decided to order fifty cents' worth of toilet paper, and the secretary-treasurer figured that he could hand tool a couple of suitable holders. He also teased them a bit by saying, "Gentlemen, you may not know it, but the only minutes I have recorded so far are about toilet paper. I wonder how our children will take it when they read these minutes twenty-five years from today?"

The store-bought toilet tissues eventually arrived and proved to be a real boon for the students. In fact, the paper was disappearing at such an alarming rate that the trustees, realizing they had underbudgeted on this "hot" item, instructed me to institute some ways of reducing the wanton waste. I did. But the frittering continued. The children had discovered many other uses for the tissues besides the traditional one. They cleaned their pen nibs with it, used it as a handkerchief or a towel, bandaged their cut fingers with it, bundled their coins in it, and marked the bases on the ball diamond with it. Everywhere I looked, there appeared to be new places for the toilet tissues. Yet I didn't feel that even these novel uses would account for the large amounts that were disappearing. There must be some other explanation.

Then one day I was able to solve the mystery. I was looking out the window of the teacherage when I saw something going on that was hard to believe. There was a strip of toilet paper extending all the way from the outhouse, across the school yard, and down into a gopher hole. Not only that, but the paper was slithering, twitching, and snaking along on its own, and disappearing down the hole. Some unseen nether force was pulling on the free end and unrolling the toilet paper from its spool in the outhouse.

Once I got over my start, I knew instantly that it was the gophers that had been pilfering the toilet tissues. The rodents were clever enough to know that the soft, fluffy, absorbent tissues were an ideal lining for their sleeping chambers. Apparently, the inquisitive creatures had discovered that it was a simple matter to tear a sheet from the convenient roller. All they had to do was grasp the free end with their teeth or claws, give a sharp tug, and the sheet ripped off as neat as a whistle, just as the manufacturer had planned and hoped it would. All in all, things were working out very well for the ingenious gophers. The strands of toilet paper were a manageable size, easy to carry into the burrow, just ideal for tucking purposes. It was too bad the manufacturer produced the odd roll of toilet paper that refused to tear easily. Such a slip led to the end of the mystery.

The "in" outhouse

The rural school outhouses of the early days are best forgotten, but they intrude among other, more pleasant, memories and serve to remind the oldtimer of the comfort and even luxury which present-day students enjoy.

"THE CANADIAN CAR"

CENTRAL GARAGE
SALES AND SERVICE
T. C. HARLEY - PROP.
HANNA, ALTA.

PHONE 102

July 6 1932

This is to certify
that we received and
destroyed one thousand
seven hundred and
twenty five gopher
tails turned in by
Miss Muriel Kendall
of Sunnynook

Central Garage
Ford Dealers
HANNA - ALTA.

Per A McTurk

"VALUE FAR ABOVE THE PRICE"

The separate outdoor toilets set somewhere beside the horse barn were unsanitary, malodorous, and very poorly constructed "conveniences." In the winter, if a student asked to leave the room, the teacher knew it was from dire necessity, and no time was lost on the round trip.

The problem of the lack of comfortable and hygienic lavatories was not considered too critical. It was just a way of pioneer living. This pragmatic attitude, combined with economic considerations, resulted in only one-tenth of the rural schools opting for indoor chemical toilets. Besides, the newfangled conveniences did not always prove to be entirely satisfactory. They required a type of squeamish attention that few student-caretakers or teachers cared to provide. So it was not surprising that some schools installed indoor chemical toilets rather optimistically and, a few years later, just as enthusiastically dismantled them and reverted to the outdoor variety.

The Balmae S.D. 2740 (Arelee, Saskatchewan) was one such vacillating school district. When the school first began operating in 1911, outdoor privies were erected according to a plan approved by the Department of Education. Then in 1918, when a new furnace was being installed, the trustees decided that it was an opportune time to provide inside toilet accommodations as well. However, the chemical toilets did not prove to be too satisfactory and within five years the Balmae school trustees were discussing plans to restore the outdoor facilities. Once the two outside privies had been resurrected, they remained in use until the school closed for good in 1944.

The matter of suitable and sanitary privies was always a problem in rural schools in spite of the continual flood of censure, of results of surveys, and of instructions from the Department of Education and the Department of Public Health about how to improve conditions.

A Survey of Education in the Province of Saskatchewan, written by H. W. Foght in 1918, stated:

All in all, the matter of sanitary privies in rural schools is a serious one. So far, Saskatchewan has failed to meet the best requirements. It is well to bear in mind, too, that whatever of viciousness may crop out in school can usually be traced to unsanitary, indecent toilets. Teachers are ofttimes careless in these matters or a false modesty keeps them from doing their duty.[1]

In May, 1929, the Department of Public Health in Alberta sent the following information to every school in the province:

All toilets should be well ventilated and lighted and should be so constructed as to render them positively fly-proof. Two sizes and heights of seats should be provided to meet the requirements of the smaller and larger pupils.

Separate urinals should be provided in the boys' toilet.

From the school environment, the child should not only learn no bad habits and catch no disease, but should be so taught and generally impressed with the sanitary arrangements of his school as to become a champion of the cause of health at home. It should be the concern of every parent to see that the school is a model of sanitary appointments.[2]

1. H. W. Foght, *A Survey of Education in the Province of Saskatchewan* (Canada: King's Printer, 1918).
2. Malcolm R. Bow, Deputy Minister, "Rural Sanitation," *Alberta Public Health Bulletin,* Provincial Department of Public Health (May 1929): 10.

Chapter Three

Tools of the Trade

The Search for the Perfect Desk

No matter how well the artisans did their job in designing school desks, students always detected and exploited any flaws. In fact, this unheralded attempt by craftsmen to outwit students and come up with a perfect desk is still going on. However, with so many new, fantastic structural materials available today, the victory is slowly turning to the designers.

In the days of the rural school the desk builders were very proud of their sloping desk tops, which were about half an inch thick and beautifully varnished. Unfortunately, such a glossy writing surface proved to be too tempting; students invariably scratched, carved, or tattooed names, initials, designs, and drawings on the shiny surface.

As the years went by, many hands retraced the original hieroglyphics and made them deep and enduring. Teachers soon discovered that the first marks made on the desk were the all-important ones, and if the guilty youngster was not spotted there and then, all would be lost. The next pupil could always protect his innocence by saying, "The carving was already there when I moved into the desk!" Besides, the expert desk defacers knew how to "age" their carvings by rubbing them with spit, dirt, and oil from the floor. Staining the freshly cut wood with ink also helped. So although the desks were plain to begin with, over the years many acquired individuality through the scars cut into their surfaces.

The inkwell located in the right-hand corner of each desk aided rather than dissuaded the desk markers. It could represent an integral part of a cartoon of the human body: the pursed mouth of the inspector, the glittering eye of the teacher, the bulbous nose of a happy face, or the protruding belly of some unpopular local citizen. Some of the handiwork was designed in such a way that it could have a sordid or an upright interpretation, depending upon the mind of the beholder.

Most of the desk carving could be attributed to the boys, for in those days every boy carried a jackknife in his pocket. The girls, not having pockets in which to tote such tools, employed much subtler methods of leaving their marks for posterity. They used rings, nail files, pieces of glass, or pins of any type. It is doubtful whether a name or a set of initials on school furniture ever achieved immortality for the engraver, for the furniture itself has long since been used for kindling or discarded in other ways. And in any case the "art" of the period scarcely deserved study or preservation.

Badly scarred desks often proved disastrous to a teacher. Some school inspectors noted the conditions of the desks in the pedagogue's classroom when judging his or her efficiency as a teacher. Many new markings were taken as an indication of mediocrity; few or none, of competence.

The "storage space" directly underneath the writing surface was another area where the rural students felt the desk designer had blundered. In reality, it was a mere shelf, and students had to exercise great care in arranging their school paraphernalia on it or a slight jar would send the paint box, the tin geometry set, the pencil box, the ink bottle, the ruler, the porcelain drinking cup, the textbooks, and everything else cascading to the floor with a tremendous crash. And as if this calamity wasn't enough, these objects had a characteristic way of bouncing to all corners of the room. Wooden pencil boxes were the worst offenders. Their pivoted or hinged covers and pull-out lids usually flew

open when they fell on the floor, strewing pencils, pen holders, pen nibs, erasers, crayons, paint brushes, and often a compass, a pencil sharpener or penknife, and an assortment of keepsakes. Such "accidents" were bound to disrupt the school routine and incur the ire of the teacher. It is said that Fibber McGee, the famous radio comedian of the 1940s, got the idea for his eruptive closet from his exasperating experiences with his school supplies tumbling out of his desk.

The girls did not have as much of a problem as they, unlike the boys, made their desks havens of cleanliness and order, whereas the boys cared less. Often a prize was given to the pupils who had the neatest and least marked desks, but very few boys ever won such an award.

In time, school suppliers came up with desks that had book drawers under the seat portion or a type on which the writing surface could be raised like a lid revealing a box like compartment for books. Such in-

An interior view of Harvey S.D. 1597 (Vulcan, Alberta) in 1910. Note the honor roll, the maple leaf blackboard border, the various reading charts, and the hanging globe. Miss Boler is the teacher in the background.

novations eliminated once and for all the exasperating problems associated with books and belongings spilling out of desks. However, they came too late to be of much help to those attending rural schools.

The desk seats created their own kinds of problems. They were hard and uncomfortable despite the fact that they were fashioned like a horizontal "S" to accommodate the shape of the human posterior. The youngsters quickly discovered that these troughlike seats could hold water, so many an unsuspecting child sat down in rigged puddles.

Why the manufacturer left a space between the seat and the bottom of the back rest was anybody's guess. But it was because of this feature that the desks were often known as "torture boxes." When a pupil stood up to read his lesson or to recite, the one sitting behind used the tilted-up seat for a footrest by thrusting his toes through the convenient slot. Then when the reader sat down, the child behind got his or her toes pinched. Or some prankster would fasten a tack, a pin, or a pen nib to the toe of his shoe, thrust it up through the made-to-order space, and make the person in front jump or at least change his sitting position from time to time.

Misadventures with Ink

No one can appreciate the modern ball-point pen better than the person who, in his early school days, struggled with a straight pen and its detachable steel nib, and a pesky bottle of ink. Students of that era found these dipping pens scratchy, prone to blotting, and difficult to keep flowing freely. Besides, it was necessary to dip the pen into ink every time three or four words were written down. The nib could only hold a drop or two of ink at a time.

The better student desks were equipped with inkwells, which consisted of a chrome-plated housing, a half-cylinder glass vial that fitted snuggly into it to hold the ink, and a hinged metal lid that snapped shut with a reassuring click. Other desks merely had a circular opening in the top right-hand corner, just the right size to accommodate the standard round bottle of ink. In spite of these conveniences, some pupils preferred to set their ink bottle on the surface of the desk, as close as possible to where they were writing. They reasoned that if the distance between the ink supply and their work was

shortened, there would be less chance of any ink dripping from the pen nib onto their exercise book. They may have been right, but a freestanding ink bottle was easily overturned.

No one has come away from a rural school without experiencing at least one misadventure with ink. Many youngsters worked painstakingly for hours or even days on some special map, poster, drawing, or notebook, and then in the space of a few seconds ruined everything by upsetting a bottle of ink.

Picture the scene. The victim, with her hands and the front of her dress dripping with ink, would suddenly spring out of her desk, then stand aloof, feet astride, arms spread out awkwardly, a completely bewildered look on her face. The top of her desk and any books, paper, pencils, or erasers on it would be inundated in a pool of ink. Quickly the blue tide would disappear over the edge of the desk and down to the floor to form a miniature delta of puddles and rivulets. Everything would happen so fast

... sbet School   S. ... No ... ...
... tandard VI   Bessie Johnston   Standard ...   Iva Trace   ...
    "   V   Mary Latimer   ...   Guy Trace   ...
    "   V   Agnes Bookless   Part II   Otto Krause
    "   VI   Cora Sannes   Ernest Krause   Sept ...

The front and back of the standard eighteen-page five-cent scribbler that was in common use during the era of the one-room school.

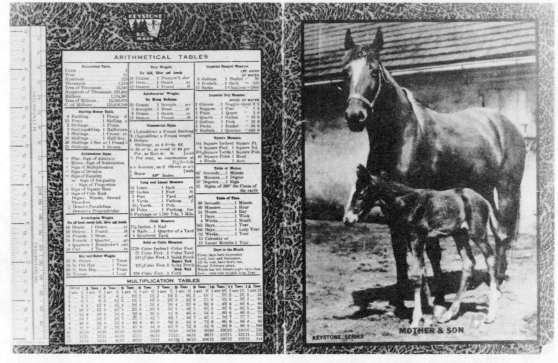

that it would take her surprised classmates a moment to collect their thoughts and start to thumb madly through their scribblers to look for blotters. In the meantime, the teacher, still in front of the recitation class, would stop teaching and tell the unfortunate miss to hie herself over to the washbasin and give the ink stains on her dress a good rinsing. By now there would be two or three well meaning lads down on the floor on their hands and knees, using all the proffered blotting paper to mop up the ink. Still other pupils would start to amuse themselves by spreading the rivulets in new directions with their pens and pencils.

The final act of such an ink tragedy usually found the unlucky girl bringing in a basin of water, washing her desk, removing the pools of ink from the floor, and mopping up generally. Everyone, even the teacher, was most cooperative and sympathetic with any ink casualty, as no one knew who the next victim would be.

If routine uses of ink resulted in so many problems, imagine what opportunities were open for any practical joker to ply his hobby. Some boys could not overcome the temptation of springy curls dangling invit-

ingly before them. If they happened to be sitting in a desk behind a girl possessing such attractions they dipped the ends in the convenient inkwell. Pens made excellent darts or swords; brimming inkwells would overflow at the slightest jar; a bottle of frozen ink, if left on the stove long enough, had the potential to erupt like a volcano; unscrewing the cap from a bottle of ink hidden in a tottery old desk could result in a student having textbooks with some extraordinary ink-stain patterns.

Children are the best mimics

Children pattern their way of life after what they see in the world around them, so they have to become the greatest of mimics to succeed. They will imitate their parents, their teachers, other adults of their acquaintance, their peers; in fact, anyone who happens to cross their path will influence them for good or bad. The following incident which took place in the Rocky Coulee S.D. 1188 (Granum, Alberta) illustrates just what form such travesty can take.

The Rocky Coulee School, in common with all rural schools of that era, was the center around which the religious, political, social, and educational life of the district revolved. Hence it was not surprising that one Sunday in late November of 1932, a baptism was held in the schoolhouse.

Such an infrequent ceremony in a schoolhouse attracted everyone. The people were not disappointed. The ritual was simple and beautiful, and its spiritual significance touched every heart. The baby girl turned out to be a star in her own right for she cried, gurgled, whimpered, sneezed, played with her lacy gown, and once in a while beamed a sweet smile toward the crowd. The occasion was not without effect on the school children who were there, for the very next morning they discussed and reenacted many features of the baptism. Although the older boys considered the baptism a sissy activity, they nevertheless mimicked choice parts of it in their own way.

Johnny Alsgard, who was responsible for refilling the inkwells that day, decided that it was an opportune time to show off his knowledge of the baptismal ritual. First, he needed a subject — a baby. There at the far end of the room was Gerald Ungstad, sitting quietly at his desk and working away on some arithmetic problem. He would do. Besides, he was so busy that he was completely oblivious. Johnny quickly picked up his full quart bottle of ink and, like a thief in the night, stole over to Gerald. He tipped the bottle over Gerald Ungstad's head and started to intone, just as he had heard the gospel man, "I baptize thee ... !" But he didn't complete the sacrament. The cork in the bottle popped out, and there sat a startled blue-eyed, blue-faced, blue-necked, and blue-haired boy.

As water had to be carried from the Heward home, John Alsgard spent the better part of the afternoon melting snow and scrubbing the ink from his victim. The task wasn't easy as the ink happened to be of the permanent rather than the water soluble variety. By the time school was dismissed at three-thirty, Gerald had faded from the royal blue-black that the manufacturer had so faithfully promised on the label of the bottle to a nondescript grey. His face and neck were not much whiter the next morning. Henceforth, the entire school took a keen interest in their human chameleon as day by day, shade by shade, he painfully regained his own flesh color. Painfully, because his mother scrubbed his head and face rather vigorously every morning and evening with Fels Naphtha soap.[1]

Important to the Point of Folly

Nothing in education has lost its former prestige more than the readers. These books, provided free by the Department of Education, were practically the only textbooks in the hands of the children below grade six. The pupils started with the primer in grade one, and then went on to study the First Reader, Second Reader, Third Reader, Fourth Reader, and so on, until they completed grade eight. Down through the years the series of readers changed, and most oldsters can remember the Alexandra series, the Highroads to Reading series, or the Canadian Readers.

All school work seemed to center around the reader, whether it was silent reading, oral reading, literature, memorization, the story hour, topics for composition, or even exercises for grammar. Anywhere the stu-

1. Leah Poelman, "Story of Rocky Coulee," in *Leavings by Trail, Granum by Rail,* Granum History Committee (Calgary: Friesen Printers, 1977), 121.

For over a quarter of a century, Canadians learned to read and to study literature in grades one to seven from a series of two readers, The Alexandra Readers and The Canadian Readers. They were followed for five years by the Highroads to Reading series. By 1936 the single-reader method had given way to a system that used a variety of readers for each grade.

Reading lessons from the Primer of the Alexandra Reader, 1914. The Alexandra Readers were used by the departments of education in Alberta, Saskatchewan, Manitoba, and British Columbia.

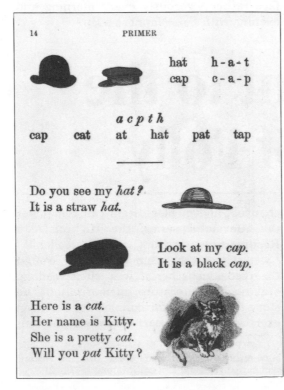

dents went, the readers went with them. The day that the beginner brought home his first reader was a time to be treasured and remembered by his entire family. Today readers are prized collector's items.

Those readers could not be described as attractive by modern standards. Their few illustrations were in black and white, and even the hard cover was finished in a drab brown or dull gray. The material contained in the readers was for the most part macabre in nature, although there were some selections from the classics and a few by Canadian authors. The poems in particular were mainly of death, disaster, and misadventure, with a sprinkling of patriotic themes.

It seems almost tragic that a book that was the very heart of the educational process should, like the one-horse shay, become extinct so quickly and completely. However, there is one consolation for the traditionalist: It took a host of books to replace the "one" little reader.

Shortcuts have a way of leading people astray. At least, one did for Irma Torie and her brother Gordon, two primary-grade pupils attending the Kleskun Lake S.D. 2743 (Grande Prairie, Alberta) in 1925. Their father usually drove them to and from school, with either an old car or the horse and buggy. However, one day in September when he was too busy harvesting, there was no one available to pick up the children, so they were told to walk the three miles home by themselves.

Curiosity got the better of them when they were taking a shortcut through a wooded valley and came across their neighbor's open well. Their father and Mr. Morken had warned them many times to stay away from the well for fear they would fall in. But Gordon, the elder, just had to explore. As the well had a three-foot log barrier around its outer perimeter, they were too short to peer down into the intriguing interior. But Gordon soon found a way of scaling the logs to have his look. Irma wanted to look too. So she set the reader that she had been carrying in her hand on the top railing and attempted to clamber up the logs. In her struggle to climb and hang on at the same time, her elbow nudged the reader and sent it hurtling into the water six feet below. She was terrified! What would her parents say and do? Worse, there was still the dour teacher to face!

As they didn't have a hope of retrieving

the all-important reader by themselves, they walked the half mile back to the neighbor's farm, to tell Mr. Morken of their misfortune. All the way there, Irma kept thinking, "The reader will become water-logged and sink to the bottom of the well. What then!"

Mr. Morken tried to reassure them that the book wouldn't be too badly damaged. They quickly returned to the well with a rope and bucket, and without too much difficulty fished out the sodden reader. He told them to take it home and ask their mother to iron the pages.

Irma cried all the way home, as well as many times during the evening before she went to bed. Her parents, realizing how hard she was taking the unfortunate incident, spared her some of the punishment for being so negligent that she otherwise would certainly have received.

Her mother soaked up most of the moisture from the reader with a towel, and then placed the book on its edge on the warming oven of the wood-burning stove. Every few minutes somebody had to separate the pages to prevent them from sticking together. When the book was almost dry, Irma's mother ironed each page carefully. Her ministrations didn't seem to do much good; the reader retained its various bumps and dimples.

The next morning Mr. Torie phoned the teacher and explained what had happened to the reader. He was also able to convince the teacher of his daughter's terror of the anticipated punishment. As a result of this conversation, once at school Irma was admonished leniently and told to be more careful in the future.

In the early days children could start school in the spring, and when ready could be promoted to the next grade. So it was that Irma Torie passed into grade two in November. The water stained and bloated grade one reader was officially discarded. No one was more pleased than Irma to receive a new, fresh-smelling grade two reader. She vowed to keep it that way.[2]

Why all this furor over one small grade one reader? In those days departments of education had strict regulations pertaining to the care of "free" readers: "Should the pupil lose or destroy his reader, the department does not supply him with another until he has been regularly promoted to the grade in which the next reader is used."[3]

Teachers and school boards were required to enforce this regulation and to submit semiannual statements to the department, showing the disposition made of each reader and the number still held for distribution. Teachers were held accountable for every reader the school received.

Absolutely Free

Commencing in the early 1930s every school district in Canada, large or small, at one time or another, received circular letters from The Copp Clark Company of Toronto, with an intriguing message: "A Map of Canada Absolutely Free" or "A Map of the World Absolutely Free." The letter went on to explain this unusual offer.

The maps were supplied, absolutely free and express prepaid, by the firm of William Neilson Limited. The only "string" attached to the gift was that the school use the map as received, under specific agreement "not to obliterate the advertising in any way."

The schools across Canada willingly took advantage of such a unique (but contingent)

2. Irma Torie, interview by her daughter Kay Torie, 1970. In 1970 the author conducted a high school historical research competition. Students were asked to interview oldtimers about their one-room school experiences, then to submit an essay based on the interview. Winners were selected from 134 entries.
3. "Extracts from School Ordinances and Regulations," in the front pages of the Daily Register for 1919, Department of Education, Province of Alberta.

offer. A recent survey made by William Neilson Limited provides these interesting observations:

Up until 1953 Neilson's had purchased and distributed approximately 55,000 each of the Neilson Map of the World and the Map of Canada to various schools throughout Canada.

We understand that in many schools each classroom within the school had either a Map of Canada or of the World, or both.

The firm of William Neilson Limited distributed maps of the world and of Canada absolutely free, express prepaid, to schools requesting them. The only "string" attached to the gift was that the school would use the map as received and not obliterate the advertising.

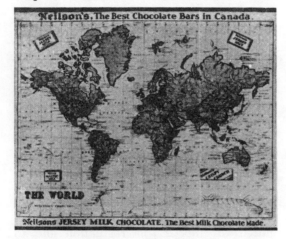

These maps also had to be replaced periodically, and they were upon request.

We have learned also that twice during the time that these maps were being distributed it was necessary to update the maps to correctly illustrate the various countries of the world as they were at the time of latest printing.

Although we continue to distribute these maps on request, the demand for them has decreased as many schools are now able to provide their own maps.[4]

Rural teachers by the hundreds have used the Neilson maps expediently, and in many schools they were the only wall maps available, especially during the years of the economic depression. Many school children learned their first real geography lessons from the Neilson maps.

Over the years they earned various nicknames, chiefly as a result of the advertising they displayed. To the oldtimer they were known as the chocolate-flavored map, the sweet map, the map that made your mouth water every time you studied from it, or the map with its oceans filled with candy bars. Yet no matter what they were called, these free maps served their purpose in the classroom most admirably. The echoes of thousands of voices of rural teachers and students resound across Canada, saying, "Thank you, William Neilson Limited, for your benevolent contribution to Canadian education!"

Since the march of progress has erased most of the country schools from our midst, the Neilson maps that used to grace their walls have also disappeared. However, they can still be seen in pioneer museums, in archives, in some antique stores. Occasionally they adorn the living room or den of a pioneer of the one-room school days or are auctioned at a sale. Some former country school teacher or pupil is usually the successful bidder, paying five times the original cost of the map.

New Every Month

The use of blackboard stencils was almost universal in rural schools; to most teachers they were a necessity, and to all, a labor-saving device. By simply holding a commercial stencil of thin paper with many tiny perforations flat against the blackboard and patting over it gently with a chalk-filled blackboard brush, a pleasing and artistic design would magically appear. All that remained to be done was to trace these dotted outlines with colored chalk and fill in

4. A. D. Grant, Director, Sales Administration, William Neilson Ltd., in a letter to author dated 23 April 1980.

any necessary spaces. Thus it was possible to create many beautiful effects from these designs. Teachers who were artistically inclined sometimes made their own stencils. They drew whatever they required on a suitable strip of stout paper, and after removing the thread from a sewing machine, guided the needle along the contour of their drawing. The result was a design outlined in a myriad of tiny perforations.

In the heyday of the rural school, supply houses for educational materials had blackboard stencils to illustrate just about any subject. They had patterns of animals; birds and fowl; fishes and water life; insects; flowers, plants, and trees; people of different nationalities; language and literature; borders; special designs; maps. During the period from 1914 to 1918, the catalogue of the Western School Supply Company of Regina and Calgary listed 903 stencils. The cost listed was fifteen cents for each stencil or four for fifty cents, postpaid.

Transferring a border stencil to the blackboard took most of the hands in the school. The primary-grade children rubbed chalk heavily on the blackboard, erased it, and kept on repeating the process until the erasers were drenched with chalk dust. Someone who aspired to be a perfectionist was given the task of arranging and applying the stencil to the blackboard. This type of work was just fine for the taller pupils, for they could reach the top of the blackboard with ease, but their unfortunate shorter classmates had to stand precariously on rickety desks or benches to help. No sooner were the designs stenciled than the would-be artists (including the teacher) took over. Using colored chalk they traced the dotted outlines, filled in any necessary spaces, and generally made the border as attractive as possible.

Most rural schools did not have the funds for purchasing such extras as blackboard stencils and colored chalk, so the teacher

Attractive stencilled borders were often used to decorate the upper portions of school blackboards. The motif changed with the seasons so the students were able to admire the lilies or bunnies at Easter, the strutting turkeys at Thanksgiving, the poppies and crosses on Armistice Day, the pumpkins and witches at Halloween, reindeer and Santa Claus at Christmas, daffodils or crocuses during spring.

bought whatever was required out of her own modest salary. This probably explains why educational research workers have found antiquated blackboard stencils among some teachers' effects rather than in old school buildings or school board offices.

Blackboard borders were a lot of extra work and had to be changed just about every month if they were to be effective. There was nothing more dull or uninspiring than to see a border of jolly Santa Clauses still on the blackboard when it was time for Easter lilies and bunnies.

Children loved to watch the border themes keep in tune with the changing seasons. Margaret Wood, a student in the -Grenville S.D. 3250 (Sibbald, Alberta) in the 1930s, aptly describes a child's fascination for this everchanging scene of blackboard borders.

Do you remember the blackboard stencils the teachers used to get? I liked the Christmas scenes with Santa Claus coming down the chimney and the reindeer at a full gallop swinging across the starry sky. How I loved those reindeer with their tiny, dainty feet! The old green blackboard at Grenville was ideal for stencils, so the changes of the season appeared before us in all their panorama of glowing colors. At Easter, we admired the lilies, the bunnies, the fluffy baby chicks, and the golden daffodils, although we always wondered why the latter couldn't have been crocuses. Thanksgiving brought us a huge turkey strutting along the blackboard ledge. How eagerly we used to watch the teacher skillfully fasten the stencil in place, dust the chalk over the tiny pinholes, and presto, produce a perfect picture. Most of the time she would chase us outside when she did the intricate work of filling in the outlines with colored chalk. The surprise that awaited us on our return was well worth the wait. Once in a while she entrusted us with this exciting and demanding task, and oh how proud and responsible we felt. During moments like these we were queens in our own right.

The border of the alphabet and the ten numbers written along the top of the blackboard always intrigued me. It consisted of both capital and lowercase letters and the digits from one to zero, printed and written. We always admired the perfectly formed letters and numbers and wondered how any human hand could achieve such artistry. We soon learned we were expected to copy these models and improve our penmanship, a philosophy of example again, no doubt.

Learning Games

Evelyne (Cates) Watson, who attended the Starr's Point S.D. 357 (Qu'Appelle, Saskatchewan) between 1910 and 1918, liked Friday afternoons. It was on these occasions that some of her teachers organized learning games. Evelyne's favorite game was a geography spelling bee.

The senior pupils acted as captains and chose the teams. Every student in the school was included in this game, so even the tots in grade one had their chance to play. The teacher started the game by calling out, or by writing on the blackboard, some geographical name. Then it was up to each team member in turn to supply another geographical word that started with the same letter as the last one used in the word previously given by his teammate. No name could be repeated; each had to be of a real place, mountain, lake, river, ocean, sea, or desert. In addition, the words used had to be spelled correctly. As the score was based on the number of letters in each geographical name given, the pupils spent a good deal of time prior to each Friday's contest searching

for the longest names they could find in their geography textbooks. Although geographical names were the most popular in such a game, the words in any competition could be restricted to other subject matter like arithmetic, farming, or literature, or in order to facilitate matters for the primary students, any words could be used. The number of innings that had to be played before the ultimate winner could be decided depended entirely on the amount of time the teacher allowed for the game that afternoon. The team obtaining the largest total score won the game.

Florie (Hatherley) Pridel, the teacher in the Starr's Point School in 1916, was astounded by the improvement that she noted in the geographical knowledge and vocabulary of her pupils as a result of these Friday afternoon spelling bees. In describing the progress that her grade ones made she said, "They were simply marvelous!"

Marion Taylor, a good rural teacher, could keep five different spelling classes going at the same time during the dictation stint, as may be seen in this Netherby S.D. 2348 (Hanna, Alberta) classroom in about 1950.

The organ, the Tonic Sol-Fa Modulator scale on the left, and the song set to music on the blackboard all point to the fact that music was a popular activity in the Sheppard S.D. (Craik, Saskatchewan) in the thirties.

Chapter Four

Rural Teachers in Action

Pioneering with a Piece of Chalk

In a new land somebody has to pioneer, somebody has to dare. Schoolteachers have always been a part of the nucleus of pioneers who advance civilization and make smooth the path of those who follow.

Life for these early teachers was far from comfortable. They fought sickness; toiled long hours; battled the cold and the snow; put up with inadequate living accommodations; suffered loneliness and isolation; contended with wild beasts; endured the discomforts of bedbugs, lice, flies, and mosquitoes; faced a gamut of fears; and received limited or no monetary compensation for their work.

Then why did these teachers come to the unsettled part of the country to brave the inconveniences, the need at times of the commonest necessities, and the professional limitations and heartbreaks under which they labored? True, they were searching for new happiness, new roots, new wealth, and new triumphs, but they were also imbued with dreams. Dreams about the society they would eventually build in the raw wilderness. They felt they were contributing something of worth to human society by helping to extend the frontiers of civilization. No group of educators ever worked under more adverse conditions, yet managed to accomplish so much.

It is difficult for the present generation to even imagine what teachers had to endure in the primitive places where they boarded. These homes were crowded and cold and lacked sanitary conveniences, and the teacher had to take the path out back summer or winter. There was no privacy. The young teacher shared a bedroom with the farmer's children or had a portion of a room screened from the rest of the family by a mere sheet. When times were hard, teachers circulated through the district receiving room and board at each home in turn. For this "privilege" they paid a portion of their salaries.

In other districts the school board provided the "mixed blessing" called a teacherage. It was a frame building that could best be described as a shack, boasting no more than two rooms, totalling perhaps 200 square feet in area, lacking any kind of insulation. Though teacherages provided privacy, they were so isolated and lonely that it took a special breed of teacher to live in them. Occasionally, residents had to cope with perils like man's inhumanity to man, stray wild animals, hazardous weather, and destructive fires. They had no radio, no telephone, no television, and had to walk miles to visit, to go to town to shop, or to seek help in times of danger.

The day-to-day trials and frustrations that confronted the pedagogue in a pioneer classroom were enormous. The majority of the school buildings were drafty and cold and equipped with only bare necessities: a potbellied stove, desks, teacher's table and chair, a blackboard or two, erasers and chalk, a broom, a water pail and tin cup, a washbasin, a few books (mostly readers), and a register. Despite these limitations rural teachers improvised equipment and prepared their own teaching materials. No one could have been more inventive or resourceful than they were.

The lack of textbooks was partially overcome by the teacher laboriously copying the various assignments and notes on the blackboard. Every morning found the blackboards in rural schools gleaming white with numerous exercises and notes, leading to the apt observation that these teachers were "pioneering with a piece of chalk."

A busy classroom in the Horse Hills S.D. (Horse Hills, Alberta) in the early 1900s. Mr. Piquette, the teacher, is teaching a grammar lesson to the class of three girls on the extreme right while the rest of the students are working away diligently at various seat work assignments.

No group of students could have been more heterogeneous than those who attended the one-room country school in the early days. They ranged in age from five to eighteen years or older; some had never attended school before; a few, and in a number of schools the majority or all of them, didn't understand or speak a word of English; their mental abilities and desires to learn were as variable as the shade; and their home backgrounds were just as incommensurable. Teachers taught as many as

nine grades, and perhaps as few as seven or as many as forty-five students. Thus, classes of one or two students were quite common. In addition, in newly formed districts, it was customary to find fifteen-year-olds in the beginners' classes in addition to the usual six-year-olds.

The irregularity of the pupils' attendance, and in some cases their non attendance, was the rule rather than the exception in pioneer schools. Parents kept their youngsters at home to help with the farm chores, especially during the busy fall and spring seasons. The school enrollment rose dramatically during the winter when many of the older boys came to school merely to put in time. In 1919, according to the Alberta Department of Education, the average length of the school year in ungraded schools was 162.96 days, and the percentage of attendance, 58.86.

In addition to their teaching duties, the pioneer schoolteachers performed as school janitors, diagnosed illnesses, and rendered first aid. They counselled, pulled teeth, played and umpired games, cut the children's hair, settled disputes, learned to ride skittish horses, and drove to school in all types of weather. They checked horsemanship and horseplay. They decided when school should be dismissed early because of an approaching storm or when the pupils should remain in the school, even overnight, due to the severity of a blizzard. They taught their youngsters consideration for others and made sure that the basic human decencies were firmly embedded in the minds of their young charges. They attempted to instill in their pupils a sense of fair play, a love of good literature, a proficiency in mental arithmetic, a correctness of speech. And even if at times their salaries were not much more than the cost of their board and room, they still managed in one way or another to buy prizes, gifts, and goodies for their pupils on the appropriate festive days. They taught Sunday school,

The teacher, Miss Helen Jensen, and her pupils of Garden Plain S.D. 2941 (Hanna, Alberta) are enjoying their school garden in the spring of 1928. It was the year that several students had just arrived from Romania, and Miss Jensen used the garden to help them become familiar with many words of the English language. She felt that the garden and things associated with it would be an appropriate place to start. Her success was remarkable.

played the organ for church services and other programs, trained the choir, helped at social functions, and organized such cultural activities as debates, plays, art displays, and concerts. This list could go on and on. In fact, one begins to wonder how one human being could manage to do it all.

The average pioneer teacher was a confident eighteen-year-old, the proud possessor of a second-class teaching certificate earned by completing grade eleven and a teacher-training course at the province's normal school. Occasionally, the teacher was the holder of a first-class certificate, indicating grade twelve standing as well as normal school training. According to modern standards, these qualifications are very limited indeed, yet they gave with all the dedication they could summon.

A Special Place in the District

Each rural school district possessed some unique characteristic that distinguished it from every other one. Only an objective person like a teacher coming into the community for the first time could sense its special qualities. In fact, for such a teacher to be successful, he or she had to adjust to the singular temperament dictated by that community. It was fortunate if the teacher's religion, nationality, social background, personal standards, and outlook coincided with those of the powers that ran the school. If the people in the district were sportive and fun loving, they wanted a teacher who would participate in their activities, but on the other hand, if they were stolid and sober, they preferred and even demanded that their teacher be of the same tendencies.

Anytime a teacher bought a new dress, it became an important event as she was the one who usually set the fashion trends in the district. When Miss Madge Rogers was teaching in Quimper S.D. 3254 (Aneroid, Saskatchewan) in 1932, she purchased a pink organdie dress that quickly captured the imaginations of most of the young ladies living in the area. The dress was used in a play, then borrowed by some of the older girls to dress up for their special dances, and finally worn by a bridesmaid to a wedding in the city. It became a community dress although the teacher owned it.

Rural pedagogues occupied a special place in the district; besides being a classroom teacher, they were expected to be models setting an example for the students and the community in general. Some school boards went so far as to dismiss teachers who failed to meet the high standards of conduct demanded of them by the residents.

Donalda McIntyre, who started to teach in the Friendship Hill S.D. 3137 (Vantage, Saskatchewan) in 1918, learned in a hurry what the community expected of her.

This was a pioneer country with very small homes. So the teacher who boarded with one of the families immediately became just another member. I found out quickly that the teacher was supposed to set a moral example and be the source of all information, both local and worldwide. Woe unto the pedagogue who was found smok-

ing, drinking, or associating with bad company. His or her days in the district would be numbered.

The experience of Pamela Appleby, who came from London, England, in August 1913 to teach in the Hillsgreen S.D. 2610 (Morrin, Alberta) is worth mentioning.

Reginald Harvey, to whom I was engaged in England, had arrived in Canada in the summer of 1914 to teach in the White Star S.D. 2445 (Munson, Alberta). We were married soon after in the Anglican Church in Munson, and held the wedding reception in our future home, a mere shack two miles from my husband's school. We had quite a dinner, and then the guests left. I had a distinct feeling that it wasn't right for me to be there alone with a man — even if he happened to be my husband. We were used to being very careful as there were so many rumors spread around, even if we only went for a walk by ourselves. But now I realized everything was all right, and nobody could talk about us anymore.

Another incident to show how very careful we had to be, and that we were under surveillance, occurred one Thursday. That day, while my husband was in school, one of the trustees of the White Star School went to Munson and met a farmer friend. The friend said almost immediately, "Say, I saw your school teacher, Mr. Harvey, go into the Roman Catholic Church. I didn't know he was Roman Catholic."

Well, this trustee, who was a Methodist, couldn't get home fast enough. Without asking my husband, who was teaching in the school four miles away, or his own daughter, who was in school, or any of the neighborhood children, he immediately called a meeting of the school board and demanded that my husband be fired. This particular person was quite a nice man really, but he didn't have the foresight to inquire first.

At the meeting, one of the more down-to-earth board members asked, "Did we ask this man what his religion was when we hired him?"

"No, we didn't," the rest replied.

"Then you can't fire him!" advised the knowledgeable trustee.

Eventually someone suggested they had better first ask their children whether Mr. Harvey had been in school on Thursday. It didn't take very many inquiries to prove conclusively that he had been. Mr. Harvey had not left the school at all that day. The sheepish trustees quickly adjourned their pointless meeting.

My husband soon heard about the whole shameful episode, and when he approached the school board about the matter, they explained it to him by simply saying, "It was a case of mistaken identity!"

Well, several other incidents such as this happened, but we learned to live with them. As long as we knew we were doing the right thing, they didn't really bother us. And when it came time for us to leave to teach in Calgary, we felt we had learned a lot from these rural people and that it had been a great privilege to have lived and enjoyed life among them.

Thoughtfulness

It didn't take a novice rural schoolteacher very long to learn that if there was one thing which she always needed to make her classroom work more effective, but only sometimes obtained, it was human kindness. Community encouragement and support for the teacher always inspired her to put forth her best efforts. People living in rural areas have always had the reputation of being considerate of their schoolmarms. The distinction was earned and no one better than the teachers can substantiate it.

Myrtle MacDoandl, who taught in the Lillico S.D. 2208 (Delia, Alberta) in 1930, discloses the following information.

The people of the Lillico district were all very friendly and helpful. I recall many examples of their thoughtfulness, such as the building of a lean-to on the school barn to provide a garage for my new Ford car. Incidentally, to get the necessary lumber, the school board at that time decided to tear down a wooden partition which divided the playground into distinct parts, one for the boys and the other for the girls. That partition was a nuisance every time we got together to play ball. Even though "over the fence was out," it took up so much precious time to run all the way around the school to retrieve that one and only ball. I really believe that after a few boards became mysteriously loose and fell off, leaving convenient holes in this high board fence, the trustees decided this good lumber could find a better use in building a shelter for my sparkling new car.

I know that my car and myself were under the protective eyes of my pupils as well. Let me give you an example. One fine, sunny morning on my way to school, I became stuck in a pile of sand that had drifted onto the road just south of the school. I found that sand is even worse than mud. After several fruitless attempts to go ahead or back up, I looked toward the school, thinking to abandon my car, walk the rest of the way, and use our school phone to get some help. Just as I made up my mind, I saw my loyal little family, about a dozen of them, little and big, hurrying through the school gate and down the road to meet me. I waited. Soon my rescue party arrived. It didn't take them very long to release my car from the clutches of that obstinate mound of sand.

Rose (Cotton) Bebb, the teacher in the Sunrise S.D. 2079 (Killam, Alberta), started in the fall of 1928 and stayed in the district for six years. The reason for her unusually long tenure for a rural teacher of that period was that the people in the district were so considerate and helpful.

Acts of kindness to the teacher were almost paternal and maternal. The Windovers provided me with milk, while the school district supplied all the fuel I required. Mrs. Swoboda always sent the makings for a mustard plaster whenever the children reported I had a cold. She also sent an egg along to add to the potent mixture so I would not be blistered. Although my pupils were responsible for carrying water from Mr. Brady's to the school, if the weather became severe he brought it over for us. I guess I was his filial daughter, as he used to call me Sissy when there were no children around. I was invited to the homes and if there was room, to stay all night and come back to school with the children the next morning.

The Sunrise children were a pleasure and an inspiration to teach as the following incident will attest.

My efforts to teach that cleanliness is next to Godliness must have been accepted, and there surely must have been a born leader in the group. One day when I had occasion to go over to the teacherage at noon, I returned to find the children all sitting in their desks, eyes front, with their hands behind them. Their faces were shining from a recent washing, their hair combed, and the cloakroom was tidy with lunch buckets placed in as orderly fashion as the individual cups that hung in their respective places. To me this was a charming way of showing their affection for me. They were loved and loving children.

My Kingdom for a Horse

In the early days, not all high school graduates became rural schoolteachers because they had an out-an-out desire to make a life career out of it. Some had ulterior purposes in mind that had nothing whatever to do with education. Many a young man used teaching as a stepping-stone to a career in the business world or in one of the so-called learned professions. And many a schoolmarm, admittedly or not, was scouting around for a suitable husband.

But some ambitions were not so obvious. Take, for example, Pamela Appleby's obsession to ride horseback. She wasn't able to learn very easily in a city like London, England, so she decided to come to teach in a one-room school in Alberta, where such opportunities would be more plentiful. She was a graduate from the Southampton Teachers' College and the Hartley University — a well qualified, successful, and experienced teacher. Yet she resigned a comfortable position in a graded school in London in 1913 to accept one in a one-room rural school in the pioneer land that was the province of Alberta, just to realize her lifetime dream.

Her story of how she ultimately achieved her wish not only makes interesting reading, but also provides important historical information about what life and teaching conditions were like in a rural school district on the prairies during the decade after 1910.

My life as a Canadian teacher began officially when our party of teachers from England reached Edmonton. Here we had our credentials evaluated by the school authorities and then were assigned to schools in various parts of Alberta. I was granted a Second Class Teaching Certificate, which hurt my ego no end as I thought I deserved a better fate, what with my many years of training and experience. I know local teachers qualified for such a certificate after attending a normal school for a period of from four to nine months, a way short of my many years of university training in London.

Anyhow, my school turned out to be a one-room affair, with the intriguing name of Hillsgreen S.D. 2610, located three or four miles west of the hamlet of Morrin, Alberta. There were two other teachers who had been assigned to schools in the same general area, so the next morning found us on a very slow train bound for Morrin. We were surprised when at about noon the train stopped at a place called Scollard, and everybody got off. There was no station, no

buildings, nothing but the bald prairie, but all the passengers and the trainmen headed for a lone farmhouse in the distance.

After being informed by the engineer that all were going there to have some lunch, we joined them. The dinner was splendid, but I made the mistake of asking for an extra little plate for my dessert. I was politely informed, "Sorry, can't be done. Here on the farm we eat everything from the same plate." I then realized I was pioneering in a new land.

This idea was reinforced repeatedly once I started to teach in the Hillsgreen School. I was the second teacher in the school, as a Miss Ella DeMille had taught in 1912-13,

Pamela (Appleby) Harvey, a well educated young teacher from London, England, came to Canada in 1913 to teach in the one-room rural school in Hillsgreen S.D. 2610 (Morrin, Alberta) for the express purpose of being able to own and ride a horse.

the year the school first opened. I boarded at the home of the secretary-treasurer, and as it was only half a mile from the school, I was fortunate on that score. But since my landlord had a large family, we were really crowded for space. I did not have a room to myself and, in addition, had to share a bed with the daughter, a big fat girl, and a complete stranger. This experience was something quite new to me, and something I did not relish. I was used to a place of my own, where I could sit down and write letters, read a book, or study my lessons for the next day. The family never asked me to go for a ride in their buggy nor did they offer me a horse to ride. I was disappointed. Nobody around there walked, but I was used to walking. So when I wanted to get away from the family, I would take a long walk across the prairie. I'm sure all the neighbors saw me coming in the distance, and I often wondered what they thought of their "walking schoolmarm."

By this time I was very homesick, as the novelty of change had worn off and I couldn't get around very far or to town by walking. I finally decided to buy a horse. The idea came to me when I was visiting Vera, a teacher friend of mine, who lived about seven miles away. The people with whom she boarded were very friendly and took her anywhere she wanted to go. In fact, their kindness soon included me, for they invited me to go to a dance at a place called Rumsey and stay overnight with them. I readily accepted, so they came over to get me and we all went together.

The dance was different from anything I had ever seen before, an eye-opener for me. I was used to carrying my dancing slippers with me in a bag and changing at the dance hall. Here the people seemed quite amused when I went in and asked where I could change from my high-buttoned shoes to my dancing pumps. So I changed right in the dance hall with everyone looking on and smiling.

The bachelor farm boys vied with one another to see who would be the first to get all the schoolmarms to dance with them. As a result we were not very popular with the local farm girls, but when they found that we were not taking their boys away from them, they relented and treated us very well. What surprised me most, however, was that it was four or five o'clock in the morning before the dance ended and we drove home to my friend's boarding place.

It was there, later that afternoon, that I bought my horse, Bessie. I had to part with several of my last gold sovereigns (fifty dollars) to acquire her. As the next day was Sunday, Vera suggested we go to church, which was in a schoolhouse ten miles away. It is hard to believe, but we decided to go by horseback and give "my Bessie" a trial run. My friend had ridden before, but I had not. Nevertheless, we started out. Whether for a joke or intentionally, she started her pony at a brisk pace and mine followed. The first thing that happened was that the horses started racing, as they were used to running together. I immediately grasped the saddle horn, which was the nearest thing I could see to hold, and we galloped along until I had to "cry off" and we drew up. I wasn't frightened, but I was so jolted that I hardly knew where I was. After a brief halt we went on at a much slower pace and met the minister in his buggy on his way to church. I couldn't believe he was the minister, as he was so bundled up, and I had never seen a minister dressed quite like that.

As we continued our jog trot, my whole body started to ache and my knees, with which I was clasping the saddle with all the strength I could muster, became dreadfully painful. Vera would not let me give up, nor did I want to. She told me to try very hard to sit up straight and ride nicely whenever we approached one of the many bachelors' shacks that dotted the countryside everywhere. She didn't want the farm boys to make fun of me, and we knew that everyone in each shack would be able to see us coming for miles around and would be eager to see who we were.

Remember, we were quite young, gritty and robust, so in due course we arrived at the schoolhouse. The minister had taken off his outdoor garb and looked more like a minister underneath. We were introduced to the members of the congregation and had a very pleasant service, but I felt stiff and sore every time I tried to move in one of the small desks that served as pews.

After the service, we were invited to lunch by one of the families that knew my friend. I must explain that my colleague had been teaching in the district for over a year and was known to most of the people there. Our acceptance of the invitation meant a ride of another four miles, and I found it increasingly distressing to mount my pony and plod along. I tried not to show my discomfort, and soon after lunch we started back home.

How I ever managed the return trip I'll never know. We met one of the local farm boys a few miles from home, and he felt so sorry for me that he was ready to get a buggy and drive me the rest of the way. However, I would have none of it! In spite of the fact that we had ridden twenty-seven miles, that it was the first time I had ever been on a horse, that the skin was blistered on my knees and thighs, and that I was a sorry sight, I was determined not to give up. After all, that's what I had come to Alberta to do — ride horseback.

Before Vera left me that Sunday afternoon, she made me promise that, no matter how I felt the next morning, I would get on the pony and ride her daily. Well, I did just that, and soon could ride. I learned quickly, and within a few days no one would believe that I had never ridden before.

I was now independent and could go anywhere I wanted and be myself once in a while. I explored the countryside, and as there was no one else available, I rode alone. One of my favorite haunts was the cut banks and the flats of the Red Deer River, known far and wide as the Badlands. A few years before I left England, moving pictures were just coming in and there were numerous westerns. I didn't particularly like the shooting or the antics of the Indians, but I was intrigued by the superb horses, the riding, and the lovely scenery. Now it was all real for me. There was a very crude, narrow, winding trail cut from the sides of the banks that led to the flats below, and I loved

nothing better than to ride down it. I would often rein Bessie at the brink of the valley and look down at the flats and the winding Red Deer River, hundreds and hundreds of feet below. I was young, sentimental, a little emotional at times like these, and loving my pony Bessie, I used to imagine I was the girl in the movies.

Life was grand! Thinking about it now, I often wonder why I wasn't nervous. I couldn't go down a trail like that nowadays, with the steep cliffs on either side. If I had fallen, nobody would have known or even heard my cries for help. Anything could have happened, but I was so trusting I didn't expect anything to happen, and it didn't. These solitary rides are some of my happiest memories.

Now I must go back a little to the time when I bought my pony and brought her back to my boarding place. I received a rude surprise when I returned. I now know I should have told my landlord that I was bringing a horse back with me, but I didn't think one small pony, which only asked to nibble some grass from 320 acres and get a drink of water occasionally, would cause so much trouble. Besides, I didn't know when I left that I was going to bring back a pony. Nevertheless, he was in a towering rage and told me he had hardly enough pasture for his own horses, let alone another one. He and his seventeen-year-old son stood around watching me unsaddle, carry the heavy saddle into the barn, take the bridle off, and do everything myself without offering to help me in any way. I wasn't too happy with these people and was biding my time for an opportunity to change boarding places. Moving was an unheard of thing to do, but I was becoming frantic.

Fortunately, the man from whom I bought Bessie had shown me how to put the bridle on and how to saddle her. He had also advised me that it was out of the question to ever take hold of the horn on the saddle if I wanted to become a good rider. In addition, he told me always to turn my back to the horse's head when putting my foot into the stirrup. If the animal bolted, I could swing my other leg over and be going in the same direction as the horse. I did as I was told and it worked out very well for me.

During this unpleasant period I was very homesick, and my poor Bessie was too. The other horses in the pasture treated her rather badly and shooed her away into a corner by herself. The secretary-treasurer and his family didn't help matters either, for they did everything they could to make it trying for Bessie. Hence, it became my practice to walk the half mile to the corner of the pasture to keep her company. I would gently snap the halter on her, put my arms around her neck, and often weep bitterly where no one could see me. I remember my tears ran down the pony's face too, but I'm sure she understood I was the only friend she had and vice versa.

Now that I could get around on my own, some of the children in the school invited me to their homes. It was then that my homesickness and strangeness gradually left me and I began to feel so much better. I'm sure that my work in the classroom improved considerably, although I found it wasn't easy to teach in a multi-graded school like Hillsgreen. First, it was an outpost school and there were no extras with which to work, and secondly, I had never been used to teaching more than one grade at a time. I had to learn to budget my time and try to get around to all the grades in turn.

The new grade ones were the most difficult to handle, as they couldn't read and it was impossible for me to set them to work while teaching others. I asked the secretary-treasurer if I could have some equipment for these children, something in the way of handiwork to keep them employed while I was busy with the others.

But he said, "Oh, no! Just teach them to read, write, and do arithmetic. We don't want any fancy stuff here." Even this much was difficult to do as there were no books, and I had to make do with the pupils' books and the odd one left around. There were no libraries in those days. So all my years of training in new modern methods were of no use to me.

There was a John Neill who owned a large ranch on the flats along the Red Deer River. His sister lived with him for a time, and later when she left to get married, he hired a nice young girl called Susie for a housekeeper. Shortly after, Susie's sister Annie came to visit her, and while staying there she came to my school. We became very good friends, and once I was invited to the ranch for a weekend. My stay was really an adventure for me as I had an opportunity to learn about ranch life firsthand.

The two girls had gone all out to welcome me. I'm sure they must have scrubbed and polished for hours, and they gave me such a beautiful bedroom that I felt I was back in the city of London again. Everyone on the ranch was so kind. They initiated me into the mysteries of calf branding, and while I was sorry for the little calves, I knew it was necessary and found the experience very educational.

I would have been sorrier still if they had been branding horses. I always loved horses and never had any fear of them, no matter how big they were. But if a cow or a herd of cattle looked at me, I was undone. I could

This timetable was planned by Irene MacKenzie for her multi-graded school of seven grades. A study of it will reveal just how demanding it must have been for a teacher to maintain such a heavy schedule week in and week out.

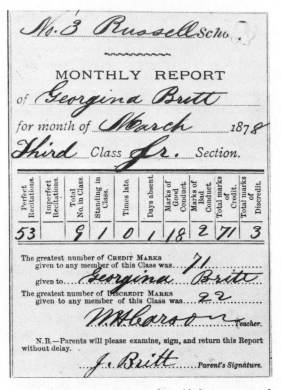

A report card issued by School No. 3, Russell Township, Ontario, in 1878. A close study of this document will reveal that teachers in those days taught "students" rather than "subjects." Emphasis was placed on deportment, punctuality, good work habits, and operating at full potential.

No. 3 Russell Scho.

MONTHLY REPORT

of *Georgina Britt*

for month of *March* 187*8*

Third Class *Jr.* Section.

Perfect Recitations.	Imperfect Recitations.	Total No. in Class.	Standing in Class.	Times late.	Days absent.	Marks of Good Conduct.	Marks of Bad Conduct.	Total marks of Credit.	Total marks of Discredit.
53	9	1	0	1	18	2	71	3	

The greatest number of CREDIT MARKS given to any member of this Class was..... 71

given to..... *Georgina Britt*

The greatest number of DISCREDIT MARKS given to any member of this Class was..... 22

W.H.Carson.....*Teacher.*

N.B.—Parents will please examine, sign, and return this Report without delay.

J. Britt.....*Parent's Signature.*

chase them on my pony, but if they stopped and turned around to stare at me, I stopped too and couldn't go on.

I can never thank John Neill or Susie and Annie enough for the lovely weekend I spent with them. When Annie and I were ready to leave for school on Monday morning, my pony had been watered, combed, curried, and even given a feed of oats — the first she had received since I had owned her.

Not long after this visit, another pupil took me home for dinner, and her mother, Mrs. Mills, asked me how I was getting on at my boarding place. I said, "Just fine, but Mr. B. is not very pleased with me for bringing home the pony."

"Well how would you like to come and live here? We have plenty of pasture for an extra horse," was her astonishing reply. Actually the Mills family had the same number of horses, and the same 320 acres of pasture land, as Mr. B. had.

"I would love to do that!" was my enthusiastic rejoiner.

Although these people lived in a shack that was divided into four small rooms, at least I would have a cubby hole and a bed to

myself. I immediately went back to my now former boarding place and explained to them that I didn't want my pony to be an inconvenience. Then I added that the Mills family had asked me to board with them. I moved out the very next day.

My new home was two and a half miles from school, so I had a much greater distance to travel. But what a difference in the treatment I received living with the Millses! They were younger people and did everything in their power to make me happy. When I woke up and was ready for school the first morning, Bessie was ready at the door — saddled, combed, fed, and watered. She had even been given some oats. My lunch was now always handpacked, although I found it hard to eat from a tin pail. At my other boarding place I couldn't eat my lunches, so I was almost famished by the time I came home from school. They never offered me a cup of tea or a bite to eat and forced me to wait until the men came in from the field at about seven o'clock in the evening. Since I had my breakfast at seven in the morning, I usually went without food for twelve hours. However, at my new boarding place, Mrs. Mills would put on the kettle the moment she saw me appear on the horizon a mile away. I could always expect to receive a cup of tea and a piece of cake or a cookie as soon as I arrived home. It made such a difference. I felt I was wanted. They took me to town, invited me to visit their friends, and even lent me their buggy when they were not using it. I'll always remember their benevolence.

Winter was soon upon us and I found it pretty cold riding horseback the two and a half miles to school. I also found it rather cold in the shack at night. My straw-stuffed mattress, out of necessity, was nestled right up against the outside wall, permitting the frost to come in and wet the sheets, the blankets, and occasionally my pillow. But I didn't mind. I was much happier now than I had been before. People were beginning to like me. A family who lived a mile away from us and had two boys attending my school suggested that I ride in the sleigh with them. They could cut across the pasture and pick me up right at my door. I just couldn't get used to the prairie winter and found some of the days dreadfully cold. I used to bundle up and wrap a woollen scarf around my head and face, leaving only my eyes showing. The boys took turns driving. First one would handle the reins while the other ran by the sleigh to get warm, and after a while they would change around. It was considerate of them to take me along.

I didn't understand the details of how the Hillsgreen School was financed, but I was certainly always worried about whether they had enough money to pay me. At the secretary-treasurer's house, when it came time at the end of the month for me to receive my salary, nothing was said or done, and several days would elapse before he would hand me just enough of my salary to cover my board and room and very little else. He explained that there was no money in the bank and that the farmers in the district were lax in paying their taxes. I never did receive my full monthly wage, and never on time. This situation perturbed me, for in London I was accustomed to receiving my salary on the first day of each month. I did not have to ask for it, nor was it dealt out in installments. By the time I had changed boarding places, there was about three hundred dollars coming to me. Shortly after, a new secretary-treasurer was appointed, and magically I received all that was due

me. I immediately bought a fur coat which I badly needed but couldn't afford.

The inspector came to my school one day, and he looked so young that I thought he was a new pupil. I had some boys attending who were near my own age, and as it was quite customary for them to come to school during the slack periods on the farm, I assumed he was another of these interim scholars. I was very embarrassed when he informed me that he was Mr. F. Buchanan, the inspector of schools from Hanna. However, I quickly recovered from my surprise, and sent one of the more dependable older boys to help him unharness and put his horse in the barn. He stayed for most of the day, but I couldn't ask him to come home for dinner as I did not have a home of my own. He watched me teach a few lessons and tested a number of my classes, and before he left asked me why I was teaching way out in the country when I could be teaching in a city. Mr. Buchanan also told me he would get me my first-class teaching certificate on his recommendation of what he had seen of my work. Finally, he asked me if I would teach in Calgary. This was at the end of the school term, and by this time Reginald L. Harvey, to whom I was engaged in England, had arrived in Canada to teach in the White Star S.D. 2445 (Munson, Alberta). We were to be married that summer, so I gave Mr. Buchanan a negative answer.

A Mixed Blessing

Living in a teacherage was a traumatic experience even under the best of circumstances. Admittedly, it did provide a degree of privacy which was not usually possible if the schoolteacher boarded with a family, already overcrowded in the then typical small farmhouse. However, teacherages were lonely and isolated domiciles. And their tenants endured a lack of such amenities as storm windows, a basement, a proper foundation, screens on the doors and win-

dows, or insulation of any kind between the walls. The outdoor privy with its swarm of flies, its pit of loathsome wriggling worms, its malodors, its squalidness, and the inevitable drifts of snow or layers of hoarfrost that frequently covered the service bench during the wintertime was most uncomfortable and unsanitary.

In addition to all these petty inconveniences, there were the more sinister ones that could endanger the very being of the teacher who dared to live alone: a sudden serious illness, a criminal on the loose, foolhardy self-styled suitors, bothersome drunks, irate parents, or even some wild animal that would happen to stray unto the schoolyard during the night. Yet in spite of all these disadvantages, the teacherages played an important role in the days of the country schoolhouse. It is fortunate that a

A small rural high school dormitory at Watts, Alberta, in 1940. Its occupants were four students and their supervisor and teacher, Blanche Coultis. Such an arrangement made high school education possible for many rural boys and girls.

former rural teacher like Blanche Coultis of Brooks, Alberta, is willing to share her experiences of living in country teacherages and small rural dormitories. She describes a way of life that has all but disappeared.

Of the ten years I spent in rural schools, I lived for seven of them in rural teacherages and for two as supervisor of very small dormitories. I started to teach in 1934 and became very familiar with the rural teacherages of the 1930s and the 1940s. They were usually one- or two-room "shacks" located right in the schoolyard. While convenient to the school, their isolation presented their tenants with problems of transportation, water supply, obtaining groceries and mail, and heating. Many teachers lived alone, but I was fortunate to have a sister or a high school student with me. Coping with coal stoves, baking one's own bread at times, eating frozen vegetables, painting and repairing the teacherage, and doing the school janitorial work were all part of the game. Despite the many problems, memories remain of the neighbors' concern for the young teacher living alone, of their delivery of groceries and mail, and of their welcome invitations to spend a winter weekend in their warm homes, often at house parties.

My first teacherage was at Brown S.D. 4617, eighteen miles west of Pollockville, Alberta, during the school term 1935-36. It was a one-room affair, covered with rubberoid, with a slanting roof. This building was not insulated, but the large kitchen range kept us warm, as my sister and I did our homework with our feet snuggly ensconced in its big oven.

That particular stove, or my overfiring of it, was the cause of our almost burning down the teacherage during a blizzard. When my sister and I returned to the teacherage at noon one stormy day, we found the wall behind the stove on fire. In a trice I dumped the coal from the coal scuttle I was carrying, and we used it to scoop up snow from a snowdrift just outside the front door. We managed to put out the fire by dousing it with this snow. I can tell you that it was a very close call.

Obtaining water was a major problem for us during our stay at the Brown teacherage. The source of supply was a well half a mile away. My sister and I took turns carrying a bucket a day after school. This water probably would not have passed a health test as it had a bad odor and left a red sediment in the pail. Washing our clothes was often done at our home on weekends. In winter we used snow water. I will always remember a beautiful spring day when we washed our clothes beside the Bullpound Creek, a mile away from the teacherage, heating the water on a camp fire. We finished our work by bathing in the creek.

The teacherage became a sickroom when someone got hurt or when an ill student had to wait for transportation home. When a social function was held in the schoolhouse, I became both guest and hostess. Babies and young children were bedded down in the teacherage while the parents danced and the boiler of coffee bubbled away on the big range.

The next year, 1936-37, I changed to the Connorsville School about twelve miles northwest of Brown, where a sister and another high school student lived with me in a two-room teacherage. This run-down building had just been moved into the schoolyard, and it was left to us to fix it up. Brown building paper was supplied for us to use. I remember attacking the ceiling in the bedroom alone on a Saturday. The long strip of heavy paper would keep falling down behind me as I attempted to stick it to the ceiling. Finally, in desperation, I slashed the strip in two and managed to make the half strips stay on. The method worked and I finished papering the ceiling alone. From then on, we could lie in bed and trace the uneven overlapping line that spread across the ceiling. I always felt guilty.

Since there were two lively high school students with me, the teacherage became a gathering place for the young people of the district. That was also the year of my first radio. Several people came regularly to listen to their favorite programs. Lux Radio Theatre on Monday evenings became a ritual for us and for a mother and her young daughters who lived in a nearby shack.

I remember one of the worst "black blizzards" that struck the district in the spring of 1937. We had gone on a little picnic to some trees, perhaps a mile from the school. This storm abruptly transformed a

The teacherage at Sunrise S.D. 2079 (Killam, Alberta) in 1928, when it became a popular gathering place for the young people in the district. Under the direction of the teacher, Miss Rose Cotton, this two-room shack served as a library, a music salon, a games room, a makeup or rehearsal station for the drama club, or just a place to talk over your problems.

lovely spring day into a swirling mass of biting sand and wind so strong that we were barely able to walk against it. The barbed wire crackled with sparks as we rolled on our stomachs to get under the fences to take shortcuts through the fields. Back at our teacherage the force of the wind had separated some of the stovepipes. When I stood

This teacherage certainly deserves the title of the little teacherage on the prairie. *During its lifetime of forty years it was used as a teacherage in four different school districts centering on Oyen, Alberta, namely, Mericourt S.D. 3963, Cappon S.D. 2811, Fairacres S.D. 2535, and Esther S.D. 4038.*

on a chair and tried to push them together again, an electric shock knocked me to the floor.

The third teacherage was at the Vetford School (now in the Hanna Museum) in the ranching country twenty miles east of Cessford, Alberta. I spent two years there (1937-39) with another sister in a tiny two-room teacherage that was well built and nicely furnished. The kitchen was so small that I could sit at the table and easily reach the stove, the cupboard, and the water barrel. We even had a fence-line telephone connecting us with the home of the chairman of the Berry Creek School Division No. 1, Mr. J. H. Hannaford. This unique telephone system was the brainchild of Mr. Hannaford. It had a big radio horn for its mouthpiece, and one had to shout very loudly into it to be heard at the other end. We felt good to have a connection with another home in the district where the ranches were so far apart.

Those were heavy snow years; yet we managed to get to the isolated homes on weekends throughout the winter. Once I misunderstood such an invitation and was busy with a batch of dough when a student arrived Saturday morning in a sleigh to take us to his home four miles away through deep snow. That resourceful lad assured us that we could take the dough with us. We packed it into a box with heated sadirons and wrapped the whole package in a heavy lap robe. We arrived safely at our destination despite the subzero weather and our sensitive cargo. The bread even tasted extra good. We had a lovely weekend, despite the fact that our potatoes froze during our absence.

In 1937 carloads of relief supplies came to our area: apples, cheese, and dried beans from Ontario and fish from the Maritimes. As many of the ranchers did not care for the dried cod and herring, we received generous gifts of fish with which we performed many culinary experiments. Some even proved successful. I also made a dish of baked beans every week throughout that winter.

After spending a year at the University of Alberta, the Sullivan Lake School Board appointed me to senior rooms in their jurisdiction, so I spent a year at Watts in a one-room high school and three years in a centralization that had been set up at Scapa. At Scapa I had the privilege of sharing the teacherage with a very fine veteran teacher, Dorothy Cook. She was an indefatigable English walker, and soon had unwilling me walking with her all over the district and even to the next school to visit the teacher there. Otherwise, I stayed in Scapa during these war years; even trips to the nearby town of Hanna were rare. Such an uneventful existence provided me with many quiet weekends during which I could study for summer school without distractions.

The Scapa teacherage was one big room in the basement of the junior school building. I found this abode warm and convenient, although very dusty, as the coal bin was in the basement too. Mrs. Cook and I were responsible for doing the janitorial work in our respective classrooms. Hence I tended the fires in my senior room, a small separate building which had been newly painted. I shall always remember a day in late winter when Daylight Saving Time was first introduced during the war. That morning I had made up the fire in the small heater, almost in the dark, and then left for breakfast. When I checked an hour later, the schoolroom was still dark, but this time because it was full of dense smoke. There was no fire, but for the whole hour that I had been away, smoke had poured into the room because I had not noticed that I had dislodged the stovepipe during a vigorous shake of the grates in the dark. The pupils willingly agreed to wash the smoke-stained walls, but we could not restore them to their pretty apple green color. The junior room pupils sniffed and called us cured hams.

As part of their war effort, the pupils in the Scapa School collected salvage, such things as rubber tires, lead scraps, prune pits, and toothpaste tubes. I remember the ants and other crawling things that scurried around in the old tires stacked in the anteroom and still get the shivers.

I spent two years as supervisor of small rural dormitories, first at Watts in 1940-41, and later at Cessford. Four girls stayed with me at Watts in two big rooms of the old Gresch house. All our beds, one for each of us, were lined up in the same room in true dormitory style. We had a regular routine for meal preparation and washing up. Families received credit for any food they contributed. One family had a marvelous crop of everbearing strawberries and sent a dishpanful of them every week. However, enthusiasm for strawberries soon waned.

On the day the high school inspector visited the school, there happened to be very little ready. Nevertheless, I proudly invited Mr. W. E. Frame to have lunch with us, and the girls hurriedly opened some canned food. Over a rather meagre meal, Mr. Frame enthusiastically described to us the city of New York, where he had recently taken a course.

The lively "dormites" had a passion for moving the furniture around so I came to expect changes. Then measles hit us, leaving only one girl and me as the sole occupants of the dormitory. This girl declared that she disliked all the changes that had been made and immediately moved the furniture back to its original position.

At Cessford I was back in my own home district. A small two-storey dormitory, plus a shack for the boys, housed nine of us, including my youngest sister and two brothers. We had two very capable high school girls who made the housekeeping go like clockwork. They had lunch planned ahead and in a matter of minutes had a hot meal on the table at noon. With everyone helping, the dishes were all washed in record time. We all went home on weekends. Homework, I'm glad to report, was done without too much protest.

The dormitory was operated like a cooperative business, with the families providing the food. In order to simplify the bookkeeping, they put prices on it. I remember that the money paid for food amounted to about thirty-five cents per person per day in 1946. The coal was supplied free by the school board.

There were various other dormitories, big and small, in our sparsely settled area of southeastern Alberta before the days of the school bus. I think back to the fine students who took advantage of living in these tiny dormitories and were able to obtain their grade twelve in some one-room rural high school and to go on to further their education. No wonder such dormitories hold a significant place in the history of rural education in our country. I am glad to have been part of them.

In most rural schools there was an understanding between the school board and the teacher that when a community group used the schoolhouse for a concert, a meeting, a dance, a play, or for any other similar activity, it had the right to use the kitchen in the teacherage for preparing lunches and making coffee. No doubt such a practice must have created some inconvenience for the teachers, but none were ever heard to complain.

Teacherages were strictly out of bounds for all children, but on a very cold or stormy day when only the pupils that lived nearby could come, most teachers vacated the frigid classroom and held their lessons around the table in the kitchen. During the months of May and June when the grade eights were given some extra coaching to prepare them for the departmental examinations, it was the practice to hold the sessions after school or on Saturday in the teacherage. The bed in the teacherage was also handy for the pupil who had been injured or was sick and had to lie down. No doubt the mattress was lumpy from the many wettings it received during the dances held at the school when mothers bedded their babies on the teacher's bed without the benefit of any sanitary protective sheet.

To be sure, the teacher living in a teacherage had privacy — no house in sight closer than a mile or two and no telephone. But it took a special breed of teacher to live in a teacherage. Not many people today have heard of "the strangler." Back in 1913 this brute strangled a young girl who was on her first teaching assignment in a rural school in southern Manitoba. He cornered her in the out-of-the-way teacherage, raped her, and then choked her to death. Rural teachers throughout Manitoba spent many anxious nights until he was safely lodged behind prison bars. There was no saying when a similar berserk person might come along and victimize a teacher living alone in an isolated teacherage.

Jean (Cammidge) Rowe, a former teacher in the Knoll S.D. 2478 (Michichi, Alberta), describes what it was like to live alone in a teacherage.

At dusk shades were drawn and the outside door latched. One evening a rattle led to imaginings of someone trying to lift the latch. Actually, the villain was a mouse nibbling at the lid of the jam pail in the corner cupboard. Another time a noise came from outside the window. Was it worse to know or not to know what was out there? I pulled the blind cautiously aside and peeked. I met the gaze of an old gray mare.

The teacherage that seemed so lonely and silent during daylight hours came alive the instant the teacher blew out the lamp

and went to bed. Mice scampered back and forth above the ceiling; they scurried over and under the floor; they noisily explored the cupboards, the table, and everything else in the teacherage. Some even went so far as to manage to drown themselves in the slop pail. These snoopings were always accompanied by much scratching and occasional squeaks. More than one teacher was awakened in the middle of the night, and while still half asleep, sensed the movement of "something" under her pillowed head, heard small pantings, or felt a warm soft furry body brush against her face or head.

After the first few sleepless nights in the teacherage, such noises and experiences became commonplace, and they no longer concerned the once panicky teacher. But there were always outside sounds to augment the mood set by the mice: the whine of the wind; the howling of the coyotes; the croaking of frogs; the scraping of the horns of stray cattle against the walls of the teacherage; and the thump, thump, thump of large tumbling mustards and Russian thistles striking the sides of the hollow-sounding building.

A good example of a little log teacherage in the parklands. The new teacher in the Calling Lake S.D. (Athabasca, Alberta) in the fall of 1954 pauses in her wood-chopping chore to gaze at her domain, the log schoolhouse.

Pride Goeth before a Fall

Arthur Peck was one of those "fortunate" graduates from a teacher-training institution during the early 1930s who succeeded in obtaining a school. There were hundreds of applicants for every teaching position, and the chances of an inexperienced teacher getting one were very remote. Yet Arthur was the unanimous choice of the board of a rural school near Orion, Alberta. Why? He was willing to accept whatever salary the school board could afford. It certainly wasn't much, for when the rent for the teacherage was deducted, it came to forty-five dollars per month. And to make matters worse, the major portion of this amount was paid in promissory notes with no indication whatsoever when they would be made good, if ever. Still, the fifteen dollars cash that he received sporadically enabled him to eke out an existence. In fact, the way that things were turning out, Mr. Peck figured that in three or four months he would be able to save enough to buy a new suit of clothes. This was something he sorely needed, as his teaching clothes of trousers, shirt, necktie, coat, and sweater were becoming a bit frayed and old looking. Besides, he was expecting a visit from the inspector and wanted to look his best on such an important occasion.

It took Arthur Peck a little longer to save the necessary money than he had first anticipated. Although the people in the community were generous in supplying him with gifts of food, he still had to spend money on essentials like salt, dried fruits, milk, flour, matches, shoes, and books. For months Arthur had been studying various catalogues to find out where he could get the best bargain in suits. He eventually decided that the one in Eaton's 1932-33 fall and winter catalogue on page 198 suited his

purpose best. The advertisement read as follows:

POPULAR-STYLE SUIT FOR YOUNG MEN IN ALL-WOOL, HARD-FINISHED NAVY SERGE 13-R178   Price delivered $11.95

> One of the most popular styles worn by young men, and growing in demand every day. Material is an all-wool, hard-finished Blue Serge, strongly sewn, with good linings and linen canvas front. Two-button coat, with peak lapels. Double-breasted vest, 22-inch cuff-bottom pants. For style and downright good value, at this price, you should purchase this suit.

It was a very eventful day when the young teacher completed the order form, enclosed the necessary cash, and mailed it to the T. Eaton Co. Limited, Winnipeg, Canada, in the brown envelope provided for the purpose. One of his ambitions was about to be realized. All he now had to do was wait. But waiting wasn't easy. He kept thinking about what the new suit would be like, how handsome and distinguished looking he would be wearing it, and how he was bound to impress the local people. Time just dragged as he anticipated all these delightful prospects. Then one day when he least expected it, the postmistress handed him a parcel from Eaton's. He was so excited that he could barely restrain himself from tearing open the package right there in the farmhouse post office, in front of all the people who had gathered to pick up their mail on this train day. He didn't waste any time in getting back to his teacherage.

Though the mirror in the teacherage was too small to allow a full-length view of himself in his new suit, the dismembered reflections left him completely satisfied. Life was good!

Now when should he make his debut in his new suit? The classroom didn't offer too many possibilities, nor did his weekly visit to town, but an upcoming social evening sponsored by the women of the district seemed made to order. So he waited impatiently for this special evening to roll around.

Arthur was an instant success. Everyone complimented him on his natty appearance; the girls vied with each other to dance with him; the young men envyingly avoided him. He was thrilled to overhear one old lady exclaim to her companion, "Doesn't our teacher look smart in his new suit?" So it wasn't at all surprising for Mr. Peck to feel unhappy when the orchestra struck up the "Home Sweet Home" waltz to bring the social evening to a close. He realized there and then that his successful debut as a well dressed man was also at an end.

Once the dance was over, a number of women were in the teacherage washing up the cups, sorting out the leftovers, and cleaning up generally. There wasn't much for Arthur to do so he sat contentedly in his favorite spot watching the women at their work. They didn't let him loll very long, for one of the workers asked him to bring in some wood. He agreeably set off for the woodpile, as he knew where everything was located even in the dark. A few minutes passed and the busy women soon forgot all about Mr. Peck and the job they had assigned him to do.

Just at this instant, one of them took the dishpan of dirty water to the door, as was the custom in those days, and heaved the murky liquid around the corner of the teacherage. It met Mr. Peck head on, new suit and all, as he was proudly returning with a giant armful of wood. What a commotion! Someone screamed. Somebody else dropped a saucer and it shattered on the floor. Everyone gazed in horror at the sputtering teacher as he dropped the wood and tried frantically to remove the slops from his eyes, nose, and mouth. One glance at his sodden and soiled new suit was enough to sadden the heart of any onlooker. The apologetic women rushed to his rescue with their tea towels and in no time sponged his suit until, in appearance at least, it looked as immaculate as it had been before the unexpected dousing.

Arthur took the unfortunate incident in his stride. However, the sense of pride that he had maintained throughout the evening now noticeably withered to humility.

An Inauspicious Start

Not every teacher's career had an auspicious start. Paul Wallace, a beginning teacher in the Baraca S.D. (Youngstown, Alberta) in 1915, describes rather graphically his impressions of his first school. He wrote letters to his mother back home in Ontario, telling her about his school, his teacherage, his pupils, his problems, and the changes he was experiencing in his philosophy of teaching. She saved these letters, and today they are of some historical value. Here are a few pertinent extracts taken from his correspondence.

June 11, 1915. Tonight I have to plug arithmetic in a frantic effort to at least equal grade six in knowledge, an attainment as yet far beyond me. I can feel my imagination and literary impulses dying rapidly within me, and there is no remedy. I haven't time to look after them at all. If three of my ten scholars were drowned and another hanged, the school would cease to worry me. But providence and the law refuse to aid me.

July 4, 1915. The department here seems to be very wide awake — way ahead of

Ontario as far as I can see. They pay more attention to general education and do not confine themselves to the three Rs. Of course, in a school like this in a farming district, we have neither the equipment nor the necessity for elaborate manual training and physical exercises. But we have nature study, agriculture, and spend a good deal of time on supplementary reading. We are at *Treasure Island* just now.

July 20, 1915. I have no idea how the school is getting along, having nothing to compare it with. The part I enjoy is after three p.m. when I take up *Treasure Island.* English is my department all right. I feel as though I know when the cogs catch the wheel in that subject, but in arithmetic and grammar, I don't know whether they learn anything or not. There are so many lessons a day — about two dozen — that the work seems frightfully desultory.

July 30, 1915. The school progresses somewhat. I cannot profess any overpowering love for the children, though a few of them are not undue encumbrances upon the face of the earth. There is one boy who is getting on my nerves. He has the eyes of saucers, colossal conceit, impudence, sulkiness, sneakiness, and a never-ceasing whine. Every little while my attention is distracted from other classes by the lifting of those huge eyes, though his head remains guardedly lowered, to see if I notice he is disobeying in some petty detail for the

When the "enterprise" procedure was introduced in 1934, learning and teaching consisted chiefly of activities. These activities were intended to cultivate the natural disposition of the pupils to express their ideas by speech, free art, dramatization, construction, writing, and movement. The pupils of Burns S.D. 2569 and their teacher, Doris Ambler, proudly display the results of one of their 1938 enterprises, "How Our Houses Are Made."

seventy-eighth time in the day. What he needs is to have his ears cut off and his hair singed — the shock might do him good. He is the only child who is in danger of a whipping. He is under the impression, which he will probably carry with him through life in his dealing with other people, that his teacher has a "pick" on him. This idea is, of course, a tremendous incentive to him to be petty and pettish. So far I have tried to win his friendship and have been lenient with him. But I think abject fear is the emotion he stands most in need of. That kind of boy is usually amenable to it. So I have become a convert to corporal punishment.

August 7, 1915. It will be very pleasant to see some human faces again. The work here is not vastly encouraging. The children are afflicted with the most fatal of all diseases, lack of interest or imagination. Whatever I do is completely unappreciated or worse. I never struck a locality which was so devilishly inhospitable. And, as you may note, I am not in the most placid humor.

September 10, 1915. Just as soon as possible, I shall switch into journalism. This everlasting association with babies is certainly the road to vegetation. I would like to meet a man once in a while.

September 20, 1915. I have decided to change my methods of discipline, and instead of putting myself out to be nice, as I have done in the past, have served a death warrant and used corporal punishment. The result is that there is no more worry connected with lessons. The children put themselves out to be nice to me. I am a convert to corporal chastisement.

October 10, 1915. I sometimes wonder if I'll ever be human again, being alone day in and day out, an object of suspicion to the natives (as all teachers around here are), and a constant weariness to myself. However, it's all in the day's work, and when I get out, no doubt the pleasures of this situation will loom larger in retrospect. There are still the sunsets and sometimes the wonderful northern lights. It seems strange that God should make all these

beautiful things only to throw them away where swine drive their teams and regard them not. Oh, the hideousness of the life of most of these people! To them nothing is beautiful. They have neighbors but no friends. They forbid their children to read stories and rear them in the image and likeness of clods.

November 13, 1915. Gertrude Allan, the motherless girl who keeps house and is preparing for the entrance and a career either as a writer or an artist (she has real ability), has been unable to attend school lately while waiting for a mail order of shoes. Her old ones were so worn that the snow frosted her feet. Next mail, however, will bring her back to school.

The Browns are getting a phonograph — a good Edison — and I am now at their place awaiting its arrival after supper.

Everything is looking brighter and I feel like a renewed being. You know the difference between existence and life; well, that's the difference between me now and me a month ago.

December 11, 1915. There is nothing to report from these wilds. Nobody has gone crazy for quite a while and the next candidate for the asylum looks as if he'll last for some weeks yet. I am sleeping in the Brown's kitchen with four cats on the bed every night. It is quite comfortable. I have my own bedding, you know.

School progresses as usual. I have been getting quite enthusiastic over lessons in history and civics. But enthusiasm is a heartbreaking encumbrance here, for the blank lack of interest which greets my best efforts is killing. The problem of rural schools, and rural life in general, is appalling. I have been reading with interest an account in *Le Devoir* of J. S. Woodsworth's lectures on the subject in Montreal.

December 27, 1915. I am leaving here with some real regret. And though everyone congratulates me on going (no insult at all — "pulling out" is almost the *summum bonum* to these folks), I confess to a very tender feeling for my first school.

In the Finest Sense of the Word

No matter when or where youngsters from different rural schools met, the conversation would eventually turn to schools, schoolwork, and always to teachers. How proud were the students who were able to brag about their teacher, or how quietly they remained if their teacher didn't deserve any praise.

Margaret Wood, who attended the Grenville S.D. 3259 (Sibbald, Alberta) in the early thirties, describes a good teacher with unusual fervor and appreciation.

I remember when I first met one of my favorite teachers. The Grenville School was closed and we had to attend the nearby Vernon S.D. 3207. All in all the prospects didn't appear too bad, as we knew most of the students there because they had come to our school a few years back. The part that bothered us was that they spoke so glowingly of their teacher. Frankly, we didn't believe them. No one could be that good.

How mistaken we were! The first morning, when she came swinging through the school gate behind George Wood's driver, opened our eyes. It was crazy, but the whole school greeted her and went to help her unhitch the horse. Everyone was talking and laughing at once. I tell you it was

Most teachers employed the practice of having their students work at the blackboard. It introduced some variety into the classroom routine and, best of all, enabled the teacher to oversee the work of several pupils at the same time. Here two grade one students are working under the watchful eye of the teacher in the Morse S.D. (Morse, Saskatchewan) in about 1947.

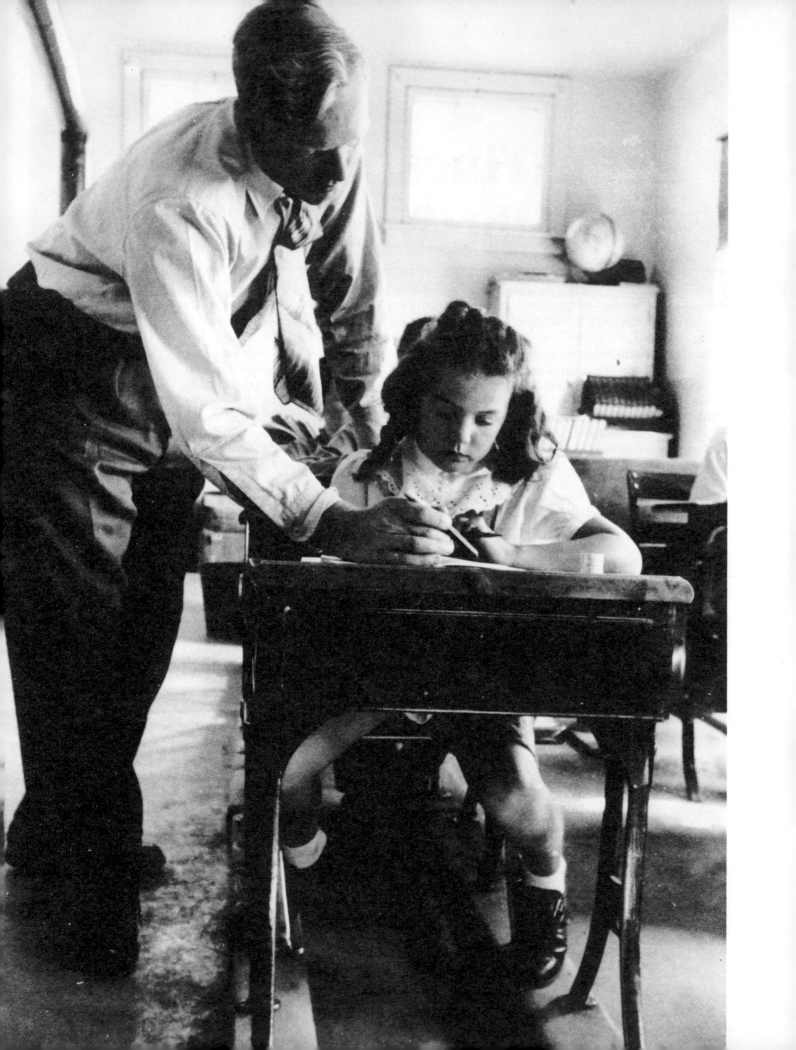

exciting. Even an old dog bestirred himself and joined the happy throng, and his wagging tail indicated without a doubt how he felt about this paragon.

That school year was so different from any other. We didn't learn just from books, but from everything around us, all the time. She used to say, "If you feel like singing, humming, or whistling, go ahead. Just do it quietly so you don't disturb the others."

If there was a fight, a ring would be formed and the two contestants would battle it out according to rules. Usually both had lost all interest by the time everything was organized, but they still had to spar a bit to save appearances. There was a time when each child had to bring something of interest to class and we would have a discussion about it. We started a collection of stones, fossils, shells, skulls, teeth, and other artifacts. I know I rode miles to pick up something I had seen that no one else had. We often enjoyed impromptu stories and special games or at times recited our favorite poetry selections. She was always introducing new and interesting activities to break the monotony of classroom routine.

She had a way of inspiring us to have confidence in ourselves and in our abilities. For years my short, stubby hands had bothered me. Not only were they stiff, but I could barely reach an octave on the piano. Then out of the blue, this teacher said, "I can't keep my eyes off your hands. I think they're lovely." You know, they never seemed so bad again.

Under such an atmosphere of learning we made rapid progress. It was a good school, a happy one, and we eagerly looked forward to it every day. It was a time when we grew up and became aware of the world and the people around us.

Often, even today, I find myself imparting a knowing smile whenever I give a quick, offhand answer to a question. I know I would never have gotten away with it in my school days. Quick as a wink would come her question, "Why? What do you base your answer on?" Not that she disagreed with us, but we had to have a reason for answering the way we did. You never met her without learning something new. She was, and is, a teacher in the finest sense of the word.

Facing page

Providing individual help always has been and will continue to be one of the characteristics of a good teacher. R. L. Moen, the teacher in the Laidly Spring S.D. in Saskatchewan in 1952, is helping Vera Lilburn with a grade two problem.

Another common exercise was recitation in groups under the watchful eye of the teacher, shown here at Aurora S.D. 1050 (Aurora, Saskatchewan) in 1920.

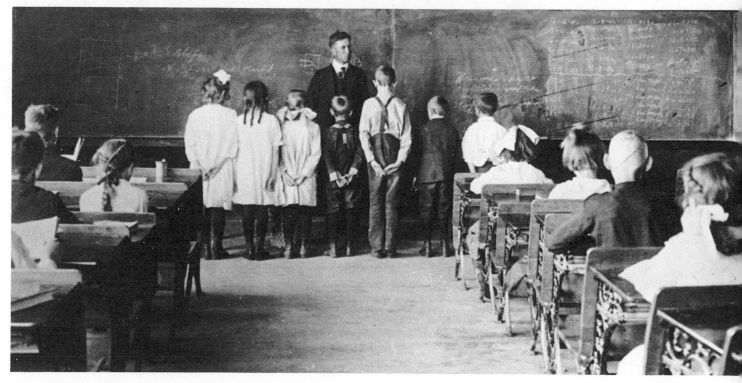

Chapter Five

Not in the Curriculum

Taught to the Tune of a Hickory Stick

Schools are like miniature societies with rules or regulations under which they can function efficiently and effectively. A generation or so ago, schools were very authoritarian, and students didn't question the rules of the school or the authority of the teacher. The philosophy of discipline in those early times could best be summarized by quoting the maxim, "Spare the rod and spoil the child!"

Teachers soon realized that boys and girls need discipline, and when other methods failed, they were glad to know that the law and custom permitted them to use the strap in the same way that would be exercised by a kind, firm, and judicious parent.

In the days of the one-room school, depending upon the teacher and the community, corporal punishment was administered for such unacceptable behavior as fighting, refusing to work, playing hookey, forging report cards, throwing snowballs, doing damage to school property, manipulating and defying authority, swearing, being a continual disturbing influence in the classroom, stealing, unchaste actions or remarks, cheating, tardiness, barn and outhouse shenanigans, cruelty to man or beast, smoking, lying, bullying, and so on. Besides the strap there were other methods of punishing the offender: detentions; writing out lines; pulling him by the ears or hair; slapping or striking him; hitting him with any object held or thrown, including rulers, pointers, books, pieces of chalk, and blackboard erasers; verbal attacks, including name calling, use of sarcasm, unfavorable personal references, and belittling him.

"A smack on the bum, a cuff on the ear, or a good thump on the shoulders doesn't hurt any student, and in this way the teacher is able to maintain order in the classroom. Otherwise he or she will lose control of the entire class if one or two students continually exceed the limits and nothing is done about it." This was the philosophy of a rural teacher in Rae S.D. 1253 (Holland, Manitoba) in 1931. While a lady teacher in the Georgetown S.D. 3232 (Delia, Alberta) acknowledged, "Yes! I admit to shaking students on occasion, or grabbing them by the shoulder and firmly setting them down in their desks. They didn't cause me any problems after that." A parent in the Rocky Coulee S.D. 1188 (Granum, Alberta) reflected in this way, "What about punishment? Well, before pupils became so fragile, a good crack with a pointer or ruler was quicker than the strap. The strap was usually reserved for the major offenses."

The strap itself, often referred to as the teacher's mace or the instrument of torture, was a piece of leather fifteen inches in length and two inches wide. It was kept in the teacher's desk inside the Department of Education School Register, next to the back cover, probably to lend some credibility to its official status. Everyone knew its whereabouts, and all eyes turned towards the teacher when she reached for it any time it was necessary for her to administer corporal punishment. As a result of this common knowledge, the strap had the habit of disappearing for short periods of time or even vanishing for keeps. Occasionally a mouse or a garter snake would be provided for company.

The use of the strap was considered a very personal and intimate ritual so it was administered in private in the cloakroom or the coal shed, or in the classroom at recess or after school when the other students were not present. Private practice was not always followed, and it was not uncommon for five or more children at a time to be lined up at the front of the classroom and strapped before the entire school. On other occasions a single student would receive his quota of strokes with all his classmates as witnesses, probably for the salutary effect produced on potential troublemakers.

Most teachers looked directly into the eyes of the pupil being strapped in order to gauge the effectiveness of the punishment. It was not a pleasant task. The student gazed back through the windows of his soul with the wounded expression of a cornered wild animal. Some, on the other hand, returned a smug and sneering grin and defied the teacher to do his worst.

If the guilty student admitted his wrong-doing and if the force and number of whacks he received were reasonable, the youngster usually accepted the punishment graciously and did not bear a grudge against the teacher. However, it was only natural to try to prick her conscience.

One dodge was to fake an injury, making it appear as if it was the result of the strapping. A youngster would let his arm hang limp and apparently useless at his side while he bravely attempted to write with his "wrong" hand. Some even went so far as to fashion a crude sling from their scarf to support a supposedly disabled arm. Others would keep their fist clenched all day long as if they didn't want to expose a serious lacerated wound, while the occasional miscreant went so far as to smear his fingers and hand with red ink to spoof the teacher into believing that he was bleeding. Then there was always the youngster who played sick and immediately asked the teacher for permission to go home after the strapping.

Edward Braun, the elderly custodian at the Canadian Pacific Railway station during the 1910s and 1920s, enjoyed repeating this story to every new teacher coming into the community of Lake Louise. As a member of the school board, he had a vested interest in good discipline.

A strapping might have produced some unusual side effects but certainly not of the type that Percy and Buster fabricated in the Laggan S.D. 1063 (Lake Louise, Alberta) in 1915. After Buster had been strapped, the two pals retired to the outhouse at recess for some self-pity. It was a very surprised and concerned teacher who watched the students file back into the school after she rang the bell. Buster, for some inexplicable reason, appeared with a hideous black eye. Instantly, the teacher assumed that he had been in a fight. But then a horrible suspicion occurred to her. Could the strapping have precipitated the shiner? She worried for about fifteen minutes, and then, unable to contain her curiosity any more, she went over to make a closer inspection of Buster and his swarthy eye.

However, Percy, feeling the game was up, quickly solved the problem for the teacher when he blurted, "It wasn't my fist that did that, Teacher. I used my drawing pencil!"

She felt so relieved that she smiled and added, "Nice art work, Percy! But you didn't fool me one bit!"

Not all strappings were accepted with such good will. Miss Lennie Lewis, who taught for eight years in the Hall's Prairie S.D. (Langley, British Columbia) at the turn of the century, knew what it was like for a student to take retaliatory measures. Mrs. George W. Radford, a lifetime moral supporter of the school and a student at the time, remembers the incident regretfully.

During the eight years that Miss Lennie Lewis taught at Hall's Prairie, many new families moved into our district from Blaine, Washington. Among them were two brothers who were splendid lads. However, their three cousins turned out to be miscreants and in time, through peer pressure, influenced one of the decent boys to be as troublesome as they were. One day the renegade was so insolent and intolerable that Miss Lewis took her riding whip, gave him a sound beating, and sent him home.

The lad did not go home. He hid under a culvert where the road turned, and when the teacher came along driving a very nervous mare, he sprang out and frightened the horse. The timid animal shied and turned the buggy over, throwing the teacher and a small girl riding with her out into the ditch. Fortunately, they were not badly injured and a passerby stopped the runaway mare. The boy received another whipping, this time before his parents and the school officials, and was then summarily expelled from the school.

The repetitive practice of strapping a child today is considered indefensible, but it wasn't always so. Bruce Lamb, a student in the Elkhart S.D. (Smeaton, Saskatchewan) in the early thirties, gives a very revealing account of a teacher who overindulged in corporal punishment.

Our teacher was a World War I veteran who had won several medals for gallantry and was fiercely patriotic about such things as the flag, national holidays, and the singing of the national anthem.

One beautiful September day when everybody was eager to dash outside and enjoy the fall sunshine, I moved around a bit as we sang "God Save the King." Actually, my feet did not move; I just rocked to and fro in time with the music. My best friend was doing the same thing. We were promptly hustled to the front of the room and received our first strapping. I remember it very well. My palms seemed to burn from the strapping and my face burned from shame.

Later, as this teacher began to use the strap more often and put more zip into his blows, many of the boys began to be really afraid of him. Then one Monday morning he announced that he wasn't going to strap anyone during the week, but would record the names of all those who misbehaved and strap them after the last recess every Friday. We were scared all week. We knew the list was growing but were not sure whose names were being put down. A whisper to a classmate behind you to borrow his eraser or accidentally dropping a book on the floor

Rural children spent many hours each day doing farm chores so at one time physical exercise at school was considered an unnecessary absurdity. Tumbling, however, was the exception. The group shown here are from Delia S.D. 3261 (Delia, Alberta) in 1933.

might have prompted the teacher to reach for his pen and jot down something. It was very nerve-wracking to be sure!

On Friday, an older boy happened to get a glance at the list and he said that my name and that of my best pal were on it. We were scared stiff. During the last recess my friend went into the school and sneaked out our lunch pails, and we took off for home as quickly as possible. I did not tell my parents and was so overwrought during the weekend that I did not eat or sleep properly.

Going back Monday morning was a nightmare for me. Yet nothing happened. The teacher made no mention of our flight nor was any punishment handed out. We had to wait until the next Friday, and true to his word he used the strap. He had a routine for doing it. We would all go out at recess and then, one by one, he would come to the door and call out someone's name. The poor wretch went inside and before long we heard the crack of the strap and possibly some crying. I'm sure that the victim didn't have a clue as to why he was being punished. Once the round of strapping for that Friday was completed, the bell would ring. Those left outside would come in furtively, quickly take their places, get out their books, bury their faces in them, and convey the impression that they were studying as if their very lives depended on it. These weekly strap sessions continued for three weeks and then ceased as abruptly as they started. We never found out why but were very thankful.

How we learned anything with the horror of the strap constantly on our minds, I'll never know. Speaking for myself, those were the years I was learning spelling, and I have never been good at it since.

Give Me That Note

No remark made by a teacher sparked as much excitement and interest as the terse command: "Give me that note!" All the students in the room would immediately stop what they were doing to watch the drama unfold.

One of the fundamental principles that teachers learned in normal school was never to maneuver themselves into a showdown situation with a pupil. But here they were making an out-and-out demand for some secret missive. What if the child stubbornly refused to hand over the note? What if the note contained some information that did not bear repeating in public? What if it said something uncomplimentary about the teacher or revealed a scoop about her matrimonial plans? No doubt about it, teachers were taking a risk when they took it upon themselves to confiscate notes.

The following incident was recounted by the teacher involved during question-and-answer period, "What is Your Problem?" at the annual Oyen-Hanna Teachers' Conven-tion held in Hanna, Alberta, November 7 and 8, 1929.

In Bison S.D. 2824 (Chinook, Alberta) when the teacher demanded that the note her pupil John was furtively folding or unfolding be handed to her, he refused. She became belligerent, but the lad still ada-mantly rejected giving up the note. Then, when the teacher took a determined step towards the boy as if she were going to physically extract the piece of paper from his tightly clenched fist, he quickly popped it into his mouth. After some gagging, he swallowed it. Instantly his demeanor changed from one of resignation to one of confidence and defiance. He seemed to be saying, "Come and get the note. Now!"

The rest of the students were startled by the sudden turn of events. All the incrimi-nating evidence was gone in the twinkling of an eye, and what was worse, there was no viable way of retrieving it. Though John was punished by having to stay in every recess for the rest of the week, no one else ever knew what was in the note. Why did John take such drastic action to protect its anonymity? The question could not be answered, for the real "proof" was safely obliterated somewhere in John's innards.

Some of the missives that teachers intercepted could best be described as puppy love notes. Incidents involving these were so similar from school to school, that variations of this classic example from the Horse Hair S.D. must have occurred in hundreds of schools across the country.

Jimmy, a grade six pupil, had attended this rural school from the day he commenced grade one in September, 1921. Peggy, a classmate, had been there for just as long. Although the two youngsters had sat next to each other, had played together, had eaten their lunches together, had worked on various school assignments together, had participated in school concerts for well nigh six years, it wasn't until this term that Jimmy really became aware of the freckle-faced lassie. He found himself looking for her smiles, her glances, the cordial expressions on her face. Contact wasn't always easy to achieve, as Peggy occupied the desk directly in front of his. A very conscientious student, she seldom turned around for his benefit. Besides, the teacher that particular year was very strict and did not stand for any nonsense. However, Jimmy found a solution to his problem. He started to pass notes.

At first they were about schoolwork, farm chores, riddles, puzzles, community happenings, and things in general, but gradually he introduced words like "friends," "chum up," and once, even "love." Peggy evidently read his notes with some interest but never wrote one of her own in reply. She always managed to make her overtures to him during recess or the noon hour without any fuss.

Then one day it happened. Peggy shyly and slyly slipped him a note, and at the instant he was going to unfold and read the precious dispatch, Miss Florendine, the eagle-eyed teacher, spotted the transaction. She marched up to Jimmy's desk, pointed an accusing finger at him, and asked, "Didn't you just receive a note, Jim?"

Jimmy tried to appear innocent, but his voice didn't sound like his own, and his squeaky "No" didn't sound too convincing, even to him.

Miss Florendine then faced Peggy, and like an attorney, inquired, "Peggy, did you pass him a note?" Peggy seemed not to hear and for the moment appeared to be studying something important in her arithmetic textbook. Yet the flush that suffused her face and neck showed that she was very much aware of what was going on. The embarrassed girl slowly raised her head, and it wasn't difficult to see tears glistening in her eyes. But outside of nodding her head negatively, she made no effort whatever to answer the teacher's question.

The teacher was now convinced more than ever that Jimmy had the note. She turned to him a second time.

"Give me that note!" she demanded. At the same time she tapped her piece of chalk on his desk as if to convince him of the urgency and seriousness of the matter. Then she added, speaking slowly and emphatically, "If you don't give me that note I'm going to visit your parents!"

What a bombshell! Every child in the school gasped with astonishment at such a telling pronouncement. It must be serious if the teacher had a mind to see the parents about it.

Enough was enough! Peggy nodded resignedly in the general direction of Jimmy and dabbed a tear from the side of her nose with her handkerchief. At the signal Jimmy awkwardly opened his clenched fist, and the teacher snapped up the limp note from his perspiring palm. Then she slowly and deliberately unfolded the piece of paper, took a preliminary glance at Peggy and Jim, and studied the note intently. Everyone in the school waited in tense anticipation. If there ever was a time a pin could be heard dropping on the floor, this was it. Apparently the note contained something important, for Miss Florendine reread it, and as she did, kept repeating, "Aha! Aha!"

Once or twice her usually stern countenance softened and even bore the semblance of a smile, but not for long. Then in a more

When nature doesn't provide for a simple recreational activity like sliding, intervention is always possible. Shown here enjoying their school slide are children of the Everton S.D. in Saskatchewan in 1949.

friendly manner she looked at Peggy and said, "Peggy, if your father needs Jim to help with the seed cleaning this weekend, why didn't you make all the arrangements with him outside of school hours, instead of creating all this unpleasantness? You are much too fine a girl to do that."

With these remarks, she folded the note and handed it back to Jimmy.

As the children walked home from school that day, everyone talked about the incident. No doubt about it, Jimmy was their hero. He had fooled the teacher, but good.

"Did you see how Old Scarecrow looked when she found out she was wrong. That was rich!"

"That was the funniest thing I've ever seen happen in our school."

"The old witch was sure fooled that time. It took Jim to do it."

"Wasn't it comical to see the old slave driver dash down the aisle to get the note, and almost lose her rat?"

"Say, Jim, what did you do with the note? I saw her give it back to you. Boy, it would be nice to see it."

"Can't do it, Bob!" Jim replied rather hurriedly. I threw it in the stove after school. Anyhow, it was just about turning the fanning mill and helping with seed cleaning at old Morton's place. I was promised fifty cents."

The perturbed lad had not told his classmates the truth. He still had the all-important note in his pocket, and furthermore hadn't had a chance to read it.

It wasn't until he reached the seclusion of the outhouse at home that he dared open the note. He read, "I love you too. Peg."

Once in a while, for greater salutary effect, the teacher asked the guilty author to read his own *billet-doux* to the class. This method was prone to sabotage unless the schoolmarm took the precaution of glancing through the note first. Some pupils were able to ad-lib well enough to alter any disparaging remarks into harmless or even complimentary ones.

Conditions were much simpler for the teacher if she managed to surprise a student in the actual process of writing, passing, or receiving a note. Then there was no doubt about who was the guilty party and the appropriate punishment could be meted out immediately. It was when the teacher discovered an incriminating note on the classroom floor, in the wastepaper basket, hidden in a book, or anywhere else around the school and then had to track down the anonymous writer that things were a bit difficult and perplexing.

Most schoolmarms were responsible for doing the janitorial work so it was not unusual for them to find out-of-line notes in the sweepings. However, it was the contents of the missive that usually dictated whether the teacher would pursue the matter any further.

It was not unusual for the students to "set out" a note for the teacher to find so she would be aware of something exceptional or improper going on in the school. It could even have reference to her unbecoming behavior at dances outside the district.

Finding the writers of anonymous notes required some probing expertise on the part of the teacher. The guilty party could be traced through his handwriting, the peculiarity of the spelling of some common word, the shape of the notepaper matching the torn spot in an exercise book, the type and quality of paper used, or some other similar clue. Accusations, unless the teacher had positive proof, were out of the question. In most cases the pupils were quick to plead their innocence, and there wasn't much the teacher could do unless the youngster admitted his guilt. Any verbal battles between the teacher and the "supposed" guilty child merely encouraged the telling of falsehoods and prompted a dislike of the nosy teacher. Such action tended only to aggravate the situation.

Although candies could hardly be classified as notes, there were varieties of heart-shaped peppermints sold in some stores in those days that carried love notes printed in red sugar. They contained such messages as "I Love You, Sweetheart," "Be Mine," "Love and Kisses," "See You Tonight," "Kiss Me," and other such sentimental sayings.

These candied messages could be slipped to a favorite member of the opposite sex when the teacher wasn't looking. If intercepted by the ever-vigilant teacher, the piece of candy didn't cause as much consternation as a handwritten note. Besides, one lick of the tongue could easily wipe out the affectionate saying, or at least make it difficult to decipher. Candy love notes were only a sporadic nuisance in rural schools as the novelties were not readily available in all country stores, and only the odd youngster could afford to spend his hard-earned pennies in such an indiscriminate manner.

Alex, a spirited student in the White Rose S.D. 365 (Carnduff, Saskatchewan), recalls his fruitless efforts to win the affections of a pretty classmate by trying to bribe her with these candy notes.

Every time I accompanied my parents to Carnduff, which wasn't too often, I made a

Like the children of today, rural students demonstrated their share of showmanship at Devonshire S.D. 3645 (Youngstown, Alberta) in 1928.

special effort to buy some colored peppermint candies with smart sayings printed on them in red sugar. I wanted to impress a girl who sat across from me in school.

I would select the candies with the most lovesick messages and pass one at a time to her when the teacher wasn't looking in our direction. I reasoned that by using such a one-by-one method, she would be sure to read my love messages. However, I can't ever recall her taking the time to read my candy favors. Just as soon as she received one, she would pop it quickly into her mouth, give me a friendly smile, and go on with her schoolwork as if nothing had happened. She would look my way again only after the candy had dissolved in her mouth. Sad to relate, by this time my love message had vanished along with the candy. I guess I was too shy to draw her attention to the words inscribed on each piece of candy. Perhaps she knew only too well!

Anything Could Happen

Sometimes lessons taught in school have had deleterious effects. Dorothy, a former student in the Melaval S.D., recalls one such incident. She was one of the terrified students who stood on the sidelines and watched the drama unfold.

In 1927 the seat of education for a district in southern Saskatchewan was a one-room school in the little hamlet of Melaval. It had an enrollment of thirty to forty students in grades one to eight. Experienced teachers were not eager to come to such a small, out-of-the-way place, so usually the local school board had to select an inexperienced normal school graduate from among the written applications that they had received. The board seemed to favor women — a young girl, barely out of her teens, tackling her first job. And what a job it was!

The teacher who came to Melaval in the fall of 1927 was a pretty young woman from Prince Albert, Saskatchewan, named Edith Zalner. How lonesome she must have been! Prince Albert was three hundred miles away; her wages would not allow much travel; train connections were so poor that she managed to get home only once during the year, and that was at Christmas.

Teaching conditions were far from ideal. The classroom was crowded, besides being cold in winter and hot in summer. Some of the older pupils were as big as she was and not much younger. The pupils in the primary grades were often quite babyish and really required much more individual attention than she was able to give them. All of these factors combined to make discipline an ever present, nasty problem. She struggled valiantly, however, to teach each subject as laid out in that "holiest of holy" educator's instructional book, the Department of Education's "Course of Studies."

The grade eight history course prescribed the English Civil War and the execution of Charles I as part of the necessary study. It wouldn't do to pass up such topics, even if they were horrendous, for the departmental final examination could very well contain a question or two based on the subject matter. The conscientious teacher didn't wish to put her pupils at any disadvantage, so she taught these historical incidents in detail. Everyone except those in grade eight was supposed to be busy with seat work, but who could resist the temptation to listen to the gory details of Charles I's execution and unpopularity in England, caused in part because he had a French wife.

Boys eating their lunch outside the school at Pine Lake, Alberta, in 1902.

At the mention of the French wife, a twitter went through the classroom. A little French Canadian lad named Pierre was the butt of all the teasing that went on in the school. His accent, his excitable nature and hot temper often impelled him to respond to the teasing with a string of oaths uttered partly in English and partly in French. Such reactions merely prolonged the baiting.

Soon after the lesson, the classes were dismissed for their noon hour break. The teacher went to her boarding house for lunch and a well earned rest and left the students, as usual, to their own devices for an hour. With the teacher absent, this period often turned out to be a time for any type of deviltry that the students could devise. On this particular day, four of the boys, taking their cue from the history lesson, decided they would "execute" all Frenchmen. Of course, there was only one, Pierre.

The chopping block and the axe were brought from the woodshed at the back of the school. Pierre was caught and dragged to the scene; his head was placed on the chopping block and held there by the two younger members of the sullen quartet. The two older members, axe in hand, pretended to argue over who was going to do the dastardly deed. Pierre screamed, cried, and begged for mercy while the rest of the students stood around, afraid to interfere for fear they would be next.

At last, tiring of the game, his tormentors let Pierre go. Absolutely terrified, the youngster ran pell-mell to the teacher's boarding house. In tears and in his broken English, he managed to stutter, "The kids — leave me— won't — alone!"

Having no idea of the seriousness of the incident, Miss Zalner replied, "Now, now, Pierre, don't take on so! You go back to the school, but don't play with them anymore. I'll be there directly."

A popular and friendly merchant in town lived just across from the school, and as his children were home for lunch, Pierre found it expedient to join them rather than return to the school. At least he knew he was safe there. Then when he saw Miss Zalner returning to school after her lunch break, he also made his way back rather warily.

That evening when Pierre arrived home, he promptly told his father that he was never going back to school and recounted the episode of the near execution. The father was furious! He drove to the home of the school board chairman and demanded punishment in the form of reform school for the four involved, or at least immediate expulsion from the school. A school board meeting was convened, and the teacher was asked to appear. She was reprimanded severely for her lack of discipline and told to use the strap more frequently. Nothing else was done.

There seemed to be no lasting results from the incident. Miss Zalner strapped someone nearly every day, but the punishment seemed to have turned into an endurance contest. The teacher continued to go home for lunch during the noon hour; Pierre continued to attend school until he passed his grade eight. The period between twelve o'clock noon and one o'clock continued to be a time when anything could happen, and often did.

The girls and boys of Swan Valley S.D. 3441 (Youngstown, Alberta) in 1930 proudly showing off their homemade swings.

Shut Up!

The teacher in the Spring Hill S.D. (Mulhurst, Alberta) in the fall of 1926 was fresh from normal school. He was keen, ambitious, and very eager to make a good impression, so he was willing to try anything once. Being of an inquiring turn of mind, his educational philosophy was "to put things to the proof."

In one of his classroom experiments, he was concerned with how to stop the incessant talking that went on in his school. The Spring Hill School was equipped with double desks, making it easy for seatmates to talk to each other, so on occasion the classroom resounded to the chatter and giggles of mischievous pairs. The teacher was determined to put a stop to all this unnecessary noise. He reasoned that if a culprit's mouth was kept closed, the racket should abate. A number of days passed before he had an opportunity of putting his "closed-mouth" scheme to the test.

It was late in the fall on a dull, cloudy, and cheerless morning. The bell had called the children to school and they had ambled in. Barney and his pal cavorted into their desk, making sure that their shoes smacked the floor with hefty taps. The teacher eyed them suspiciously, but inwardly smiled to himself. Would his experiment with these two boys work? Time would tell!

The instant the teacher rose from his desk and stood on the platform, the room became hushed, for this was the signal for the morning classes to begin. Soon lessons were being assigned, children helped with their individual problems, questions asked and answered, work checked, and recitations heard. After an hour of activity, the teacher sat down on the edge of his desk to catch his breath and enjoy the hum of an industrious classroom.

Suddenly, in the far left-hand corner of the room, he detected a stifled snicker. This snicker spread like a wildfire and before long the entire room was in gales of laughter.

Barney and his partner were responsible. With a single stride, the teacher was in front of them. A hush fell upon the entire classroom as no one wanted to miss what was going to happen. To everyone's surprise the teacher merely scolded the brash pair and told them to behave themselves. "No, this still isn't the right psychological moment to try my experiment," thought the teacher as he sauntered back to the front of the room.

Barney and his chum felt they had won the battle. Little did they realize that there was still a war to contest. The two were bubbling over with spirits — the spirits of twelve-year-olds trying to defy authority. Everything seemed to amuse them and sporadically a sudden burst of laughter would fill the room.

A human being, schoolteacher or not, can only stand so much! So after the sixth outburst, the teacher stalked to the back of the room, seized the two culprits by the ears, marched them up to the front, and hustled them onto the platform. He sat them down, not too gently, on the chairs that were on either side of his desk, opened the top drawer of his desk, and removed a three-inch roll of adhesive tape. Once again the schoolroom became silent. Everyone stared in amazement at the teacher. What was he going to do? Stick the boys to their chairs? Fasten their happy feet to the floor? Tape their hands behind their back? No, his intention wasn't anything that simple. He proceeded to cut two equal pieces of adhesive tape from the roll and then smartly and skillfully clapped them right across the boys' mouths. The school roared with laughter. This was the funniest thing that had happened in the school for years.

Barney sat there for the rest of the day wondering whether he'd live to make it back home after school. He spent his time trying to inhale any air that managed to slip by his inflamed adenoids. His breathing became

The mud, water, and decaying vegetation that characterized most prairie sloughs during spring had an irresistible attraction for the students at recess or the noon hour. Pupils of Lone Butte-McKay S.D. 2607 (Sunnynook, Alberta) were no different, for here they have all flocked to a slough to watch one of their classmates take off on the muddy main in his homemade raft.

shallow and rapid. He felt dizzy. The large writing on the blackboard began to blur.

"Enough is enough," thought Barney. With one quick tug he jerked the tape off his mouth. It stung, but what a relief! However, within minutes the teacher taped the lad's mouth again. It became a contest, for time and again, Barney, in desperation, would rip off the strip, and the teacher, just as desperately and probably more energetically, would clamp it back again.

Rage kept growing in the small boy and by the time school was out, his rage had turned into hate. Barney swore that he would "bust up the teacher real good" when he got big enough.

"You just wait and see!" he growled.

Time passed. Barney grew. But in Barney's mind, so did the teacher. A young person just couldn't win. In his grade eight year, Barney was taken from school to work on the farm and help support the family, and with him went his resentment for his teacher.[1]

Belling the Cat

Many people are familiar with the story "Who Will Bell the Cat?" found in one of the second grade readers, but few are aware that the "cat" to most school children meant the "teacher" and the "belling" symbolized fastening any silly thing to a teacher's coattail or the bustle of a skirt to make him or her appear ridiculous. Usually the entire class was sworn to secrecy while some intrepid youngster volunteered or was selected to do the actual deed. The idea was to pin, tie, stick, hang, or affix by any means possible the queer "bell" on the teacher. This trick would provide a bit of fun for everyone but the "cat." The more bizarre the thing attached, the more hilarity it provided; so such things as a pig's tail, a giant grasshopper, a fan of gopher tails, a piece of paper with the enticing words "KICK ME" printed in bold letters, quill feathers, or even a rooster's or gobbler's head have appeared on the teacher's back.

1. Barney Peters, interview by Pamela Aylard for historical research essay competition, 1970.

One of the most productive field trips ever held in Hanna took place in 1934, when the Alberta Wheat Pool issued invitations to eight neighboring rural schools to attend a "Day at the Elevator." The students were given a conducted tour of the elevator and shown what happened to a load of grain from the time it was delivered until it was funnelled into a waiting box car. It was the first time that most of the students had ever been inside a grain elevator.

The whole affair was always very embarrassing to the teacher, for she was usually mystified why the children were smiling, snickering, or even laughing out loud. She would keep her eyes peeled for the cause of the disturbance, only to discover that it wasn't being instigated by the usual mischief makers. Soon it would dawn on her that maybe there was something "different" about her that was sparking the extra jollification. Under such circumstances most teachers edged cautiously over to their home base, the teacher's desk, to do some self-examination. As she sat down to study the situation, the incongruous lump at her back unravelled the mystery.

"Who did it?" would be the foremost question in the teacher's mind. It took some good detective work on her part, or a tattler, to reveal the guilty party. Once that was done she had to take appropriate action, not only to punish the student or students responsible, but also to provide a salutary effect on the rest of the school as well so the "belling" would not be repeated.

A typical bell the cat prank that still lives in the minds of the students who attended Moore S.D. 377 (Coronation, Alberta) took place during the time that Mr. Edget taught there.

Mr. Edget was an elderly man, and although a splendid teacher and disciplinarian, he had incurred the dislike of some of his students. First he refused to put on a Christmas concert, although he had no objection to the mothers of the community doing it. In the second place he had the tormenting habit of stamping his feet so hard when agitated in the classroom that many a pupil began to suffer from earaches. It was not surprising that when the boys found an unusually large dead mouse in the barn, it was decided there and then to "bell the cat" by pinning it to Mr. Edget's coattail. But who would do it was the big question. No one volunteered so the big boys grouped around Ernest and told him that he was just perfect for the business at hand as he was small and very nimble. Everybody agreed and even crossed their

88

hearts and promised never to tell on the victimized Ernest.

Ernest succeeded in fastening the mouse to the schoolmaster's coattail with a clothespin as he was stooped over assisting Effie at the desk in front of Ernest. Soon the smiles turned to snickers, the snickers to giggles, and the odd giggle burst into an out-and-out laugh. It was so funny to see the so-formal Mr. Edget walking up and down the aisles with the mouse bouncing delightfully up and down on his coattail just as if it were very much alive and well. However, when Mr. Edget sat down to listen to the grade three pupils repeat their memory work, he found the animal.

When no one admitted responsibility for the prank, he cancelled recess and warned that there would be no further recesses until the guilty person was named. It didn't take long! The big girls were already fed up with the inaction of one lost recess, never mind three or four, so they told on poor Ernest. All the children in the school — with the exception of Ernest, who received a good strapping for his part in the drama — thought the belling of Mr. Edget was the best ever.[2]

Punishment to Fit the Crime

The opera *The Mikado* enunciated a philosophy of punishment that found favor with many rural teachers. The idea expressed in song was "to let the punishment fit the crime." Such measures adopted in the classroom often proved both unique and interesting, as the following tale confirms.

Marjorie Portfors, the teacher in the Red Rose S.D. (Hanna, Alberta) in 1931, lived with her family on a farm in the district. It was her practice to travel to and from school in a gray Dort automobile. Her knowledge of this mechanical wonder, outside of knowing how to drive it, was very limited. So when Don Sim, a mischievous youngster, let out some of the air from each of the tires on the car, she was unaware what caused it to behave so strangely on her way home that evening. The automobile rode like a lumber wagon, was difficult to steer and kept roaming all over the road, and the engine seemed to be laboring more than usual. Mrs. Portfors wasn't long in telling her husband about the strange antics of the car. He investigated, and it didn't take him very long to realize that the deflated tires were at fault. When he informed his wife, she told him not to do anything about it. She said she knew the cause of the problem and would remedy it in her own way the next day at school. She asked him only to replace the tire pump that had come with the car with the old leaky one that had been saved for emergencies.

Although Don Sim had his shortcomings, he was a good youngster at heart and often asked Mrs. Portfors whether he could help her with some of her more arduous chores. When he asked her on this particular occasion, she nodded her head in approval and pleasantly said, "Thanks for asking, Don. Yes, it just happens that I have something that you can do for me. The tires on my car seem to be low, and I was wondering whether you would be good enough to pump them up."

Before the sheepishly grinning youngster had time to change his mind, Mrs. Portfors went to the car, took out the air pump, and

2. Effie (Moore) Butterwick, account of Moore S.D. 337, in *In the Beginning*, Coronation TNC Golden Age Club (Calgary: Friesen Printers, 1979), 450.

If a teacher had an interest in boxing, football, checkers, tumbling, hockey, or any other sport, it wasn't long before every youngster in the school was following suit and taking part. This explains why in 1945 both the boys and girls in Cereal S.D. 3192 (Cereal, Alberta) took up boxing so zealously. Even two amiable fellows like Albert and Kenny could put on the boxing gloves and demonstrate their pugilistic abilities.

handed it to the astonished boy. She had her own kind of grin as she watched him connect the hose of the one-cylinder hand pump to the valve stem on one of the tires and start pumping.

Inflating the tires with the far-from-adequate pump was hard, exhausting work, but Don kept at the task until all were road worthy. He realized that he had been justly punished. The knowing smile and the "Thank you, Don!" he received from his teacher merely confirmed his suspicions that "she knew that he knew that she knew."

Halloween Aftermath

Mrs. John Vigen, the teacher at the Lake Thelma S.D. 2427 (Fleet, Alberta), would usually get to school before her pupils, but on Monday morning, November 1, 1953, the reverse proved to be true.

I noticed they were standing on the porch and watching my progress towards the school with more than usual interest. Even from a distance I knew something was wrong, for they appeared to be nervous, afraid, and uncertain about something.

Their actions puzzled me, but I didn't give them much thought. My spirits were high as the sun had just come out and I knew I was returning to a tidy school. The previous Friday, the twenty children ranging in grades from one to nine and I had given the school a thorough cleaning. We had swept the floor, straightened the rows of desks, dusted and washed everything, and arranged the books in the library space in proper sections and in alphabetical order. The classroom was a picture of neatness and order. I still retained these pleasant thoughts in my mind when I entered the school.

Words couldn't describe the way I felt when I looked in! The scene that met my eyes was in direct contrast to what I had expected. My first impulse was to turn around and go back home. Instead, I took a deep breath and surveyed the shambles.

All the books that had been arranged so neatly on the shelves in the library were littered from one end of the room to the other. The pupils' desks had been overturned and their books, rulers, pencil boxes, ink bottles, erasers, crayons, pens, pencils, and paint boxes were scattered recklessly over the floor. My desk, although it wasn't tipped over, was completely stripped of all my things. Papers were strewn everywhere, and at my feet were the fragments of the ornaments and the other odds and ends that usually decorated my desk. The huge school bell, which had been removed from the tower when the roof had been reshingled and placed outside by the porch, was now ensconced in the center of the room. Large chunks of coal had been brought in from the adjoining coal shed and dropped helter-skelter over the floor. The ash pan had been

emptied into some of the desks and all along the windowsills. Oh, what a mess!

I sat down in my chair, which was about the only thing still upright, and mumbled something about phoning the school board. The concerned and startled children gathered around me and promised they would all pitch in to help clean up the mess. It was then and there that I realized that it was not the children who had perpetrated this dastardly Halloween trick.

I felt proud to see all my pupils go to work with such energy and enthusiasm. It is a strange thing, but faced with a crisis, children always undergo a transformation for the better. When they might well be resentful at changes of plans and unpleasant tasks, they become instead cooperative, considerate, and responsible. This morning was no exception! The desks were placed upright, and they began the tedious task of sorting out their books, pencils, pens, crayons, paint boxes, and other personal effects.

Watching my pupils making such good headway towards restoring order and cleanliness made me feel a little better. I got up and began collecting some of the papers that had been hurled off my desk. Four of the older boys took it upon themselves to

Dorothy James, a student-teacher in 1929-30, learns first hand about rural school noon hour and recess supervision as she participates with the pupils and their teacher, Mrs. Helen Tucker, of Leith Hill S.D. 3610 (Endiang, Alberta) in an exciting playground game of drop the handkerchief.

remove the two-hundred-pound bell and carry it back out to the porch. The library books were replaced on the shelves, and to my surprise and pleasure they were arranged in proper sequence. We found that the coal was the hardest and dirtiest part of the cleanup. The large chunks were picked up by hand and returned to the coal shed, while the smaller pieces and the slack were swept up and deposited in the coal pail.

It took us about two hours to bring order and neatness to the interior of our little school. When we were finished, it looked just as we had left it on Friday afternoon, except for a few coal smudges on the floor that we were unable to remove.

I never found out who was responsible for the mean trick, but I did discover a characteristic in my pupils that I had never known really existed.[3]

Teacher for a Day

Every rural school had its mischief maker and the Metropole S.D. 1608 (North Battleford, Saskatchewan) in 1942 was no exception. Robert, a twelve-year-old student, fitted the role perfectly. He had darting blue eyes that continually seemed to be searching for some deviltry to perpetrate. His plump, smirking face was topped by a mop of unruly brown hair. Even his quick temper added to his mischievous demeanor. In addition, Robert was a fast worker and unusually bright, so he always managed to find time for his extracurricular activities.

One day in April proved especially productive for the young scoundrel. He filled a little grade one girl's hat with slushy snow and then clamped it on her head. He thought it was a great joke to watch the tot try to extricate herself from her snowy headgear. During the arithmetic period he scribbled all over Jack's exercise book just because his classmate was two pages ahead of him. When the girl across the aisle teased him for being green with envy, he poked her in the arm with the point of his compass. He also dipped the end of one of Ilene's braids into his inkwell, and then made prints with it all over one of his scribblers. Then, to top this day of days, he pulled out a ball of fine battery wire from his pocket and proceeded to stretch it across the aisle about four inches from the floor, hoping to trip some unwary pupil.

However, the teacher spotted Robert

while he was putting the finishing touches to his trap. She let him finish, and then gave him the surprise of his life when he raised his head to find her standing directly over him. She quietly said, "Please rewind all that wire on the spool you have in your pocket and then put it on my desk."

Robert did as he was bid, wondering all the while what punishment she might mete out. He didn't have long to wait. Miss Huggett picked up the spool of wire, examined it carefully, looked sternly at him and said, "Young man, since you seem to have no wish to do your schoolwork, you may as well make yourself useful by taking over from me and teaching for the rest of the day. You come up to the front of the room and take charge of the classes. Henceforth you will be Mr. Robert. In the meantime, I'll sit in your desk and do your work."

The exchange was duly effected, and moments later, when the students glanced guardedly in her direction, they found her busily engaged in doing Robert's work. To all intents and purposes, she appeared to be just one of them, while the boy at the teacher's desk was the outsider.

At first Robert thought it was a big joke to sit in the teacher's chair behind the imposing brown desk and make faces at the rest of the students. However, no one paid any attention to him. In fact, after awhile,

3. Annie (English) Vigen, interview by Joyce Nelson for historical research essay competition, 1970.

It was fun to dress up like the teacher and put your classmates through their paces just like the "real" teacher in the "real" school. The children from Sunnynook S.D. 4788 (Sunnynook, Alberta) seem to be having a lot of fun playing school out on the prairie in 1939, even when the pointer had to be raised to maintain discipline.

things became untenable for the twelve-year-old teacher.

Little Nester, who often found grammar a puzzle, turned around ask Miss Huggett whether "good" as used in a particular sentence in his grammar exercise was an adjective or an adverb. She firmly told him to ask the substitute teacher, as for the time being she was a grade seven student studying geography. Nester promptly put up his hand and did. Mr. Robert replied with much trepidation that he thought it was probably an adverb. The rest of the students scoffed at his uncertain answer.

Then Ilene, who was very clever and anxious to get even with Mr. Robert, asked him where Timbuktu was located, as she couldn't find it on her small map of Africa. A questioning look at Miss Huggett gave him only a stony, disinterested stare. Finally he had to admit to Ilene that he didn't know. The class members ignored him in complete disgust, and several turned to help Ilene find the elusive city.

These efforts created some disturbance, so Miss Huggett told Mr. Robert he must keep better order. When he attempted to do this, his efforts not only proved futile but also provoked many nasty looks. He realized by now that he was cultivating the dislike of his classmates. Everything he attempted to do, as the substitute teacher, seemed to backfire, leaving him humiliated at every turn. The situation was no longer funny for the sham teacher. Eventually, he contrived what he thought would be a way out of his dilemma. He hesitantly but triumphantly dismissed the class for recess and then joined them in their rush for the door.

His dash for freedom was foiled, for the real teacher called him back and emphatically said, "Sorry, Mr. Robert, you have too much work awaiting you to fritter your time away playing at recess. You are a teacher now and must act as one. You have the grade one reading lesson to print on the blackboard, the grade four spelling workbooks to correct, and the grade six rapid calculation answers to check. Now you better get busy and forget all about playing outside!"

This was more than the crestfallen Mr. Robert could stand. He broke down and wept bitterly. However, it wasn't until after recess that Miss Huggett found it in her heart to restore him to plain "Robert," a grade seven pupil.

After this incident, whenever Robert started acting up, the teacher merely pointed to her chair. Immediately he would turn red, hang his head in shame, and with noticeable discomfiture resume the work he had been neglecting. He would give no more trouble for the rest of that day.[4]

---

4. Mary (Huggett) Chvala, the teacher, interview by her daughter Charmaine Chvala for historical research essay competition, 1970.

Chapter Six

Getting There the Old Way

When the School Horse Was King

In this mechanical age of school buses, automobiles, and motorcycles, it is difficult to picture a time when riding a horse or walking was probably the only means of getting to and from the district school. Stories about the old school horse that used to be so common somehow don't seem so real today. In fact, local newspapers in those early days never failed to record the

The students of Melbrae S.D. 2777 (Hardisty, Alberta) in 1933 are ready to go home after a day at school. Some of the horses carried as many as three students on their backs.

superannuation of the faithful horses which transported the district schoolchildren for more years than most people could remember. It is always a pleasure to listen to oldtimers relate some of their experiences with school horses. They are told so convincingly that one can almost relive their trials.

In 1946 in the Dalum S.D. 3969 (Drumheller, Alberta), one of Magnus (Mack) Poulsen's faithful horses had reached the end of his useful years. So Mack took him to a nearby fox farm, believing that the animal would be destroyed without any delay. However, he was turned out to pasture to await later extermination. Unfortunately,

this particular pasture ran parallel to the road and the poor horse sorrowfully followed his master along the fence whinnying mournfully all the while, as if knowing his fate. The people in the district will always remember how Mack vowed on his return that he would never again treat a faithful servant who had given many years of willing service in such a shoddy manner.

Hazel White describes her experiences with horses while attending Garrat School.

As I sit by my window, I often see the yellow school buses going by, and I think back to my school days when our way of life was so different. I started school in 1921 in a rural school called Garrat S.D. (Mitchellton, Saskatchewan) and instead of riding a bus the two miles to school, as children today would, I rode horseback.

I remember the first day that I started to school on my pony. We had gone no more than a quarter of a mile when the horse suddenly decided to return. I couldn't change his mind, so we arrived back home. The next day Dad took me out to the corner, and I went to school in the company of a neighbor's daughter, who made sure my horse didn't turn tail and head for home. We continued riding together until I learned the knack of convincing my stubborn pony that we went where I, not he, wanted to go. From then on, I was on my own going to and from school so I learned responsibility at an early age. I think the children nowadays miss so much: the joy of riding horseback, the inspiration of being close to nature, and the thrill of watching, at first hand, the unfolding of each new season.

When my sister became old enough to attend school, we rode double. I recall one day in spring while we were on our way to school, the horse slipped and sat down in the mud with a plop. It was just like a circus act, but not for us. My sister slid off the back end, right into a mud puddle. My coat caught on the saddle horn and I was hung up until all the buttons were torn off. Without their support I tumbled backwards to the ground. However, only our pride was hurt, and after scraping some of the mud from our clothes, we remounted our pony and stubbornly continued on our way to school.

My most serious accident with a horse occurred when I was nine years old. It was three-thirty, school was out, and everyone was excitedly homeward bound. My sister and I were riding our favorite pony named Old Bob that day. He was plodding along in his usual style when I suddenly heard some of our school friends coming up behind us in their horse and cart. I was too slow in getting off the road, and they plowed into us, jimmying one of the shafts of their vehicle right into the body of our poor horse. He staggered immediately. My sister nimbly slipped off his back, but I was still on when he fell heavily to the ground, landing on our dropped lunch pail with such force that it was flattened like a pancake. Our friends instantly went to get Dad. My sister went with them, but I wouldn't leave Old Bob. He attempted to rise once, but fell back and died in a short time, with his head still resting on my lap. We were like that when Dad arrived to haul him home.

I couldn't eat my supper that night and went to bed crying. Old Bob meant so much to me that I still get a lump in my throat when I think of his tragic end.

Horses, although considered intelligent animals, are rarely given credit for being able to rationalize. Yet in the Carlyle S.D. 3083 (Benton, Alberta), the actions of a school horse in the winter of 1926 prompted district residents to say, "Yes, Lady can think!"

Lloyd Anderson was on his way home from the Carlyle School on a mild, snowy day, riding Lady, his thoroughbred black mare. Then, as so often happens on the

prairie, a wind came up, and in a matter of minutes, the gentle, fleecy flakes had turned into a swirling mass of cold, biting sleet. It became so thick it was hard for Lloyd to see. He didn't know whether to go on home or return to the school. He realized that he must be near Pumpkin Hill, where he would be able to get his bearings. But all the seven-year-old lad was able to do was to gaze into the blinding whiteness, and all directions seemed the same to him. He knew he was lost.

Lady was becoming impatient with his apparent confusion, and the only thing he could think of was to give her a free rein and let her find the way. She didn't hesitate a moment, and away they went. A few minutes later the lad received a rude surprise when he discovered that instead of facing the blizzard as they had been doing since leaving school, they were now going with it. He hadn't a clue where he was, or where he was going. His only consolation was that Lady was still taking the rein and seemed to be determined to carry him somewhere. He didn't dare check her, but encouraged her

These three little girls are homeward bound from the Poplar Dale S.D. (Dapp, Alberta). Their lunch pails, symbolic of the rural student, are gleaming in the setting sun.

Shown here is the interior of Spondin S.D. 3375 after the 1937 blizzard. The Waterman-Waterbury furnace had to stand idly by for hours until the fine snow had been carefully dusted from everything and then swept outside.

In some areas, rural school districts joined together to form what was known as a consolidated school district. They used their combined resources to construct a large central school and then transported the students by horse-drawn vans. They felt that their children would receive a better education, including the opportunity to take high school, at a cost not much more than if they had built and operated their own one-room schools. A good example of such a consolidation was the Melita Consolidated School (Melita, Manitoba) in 1915. One of the participating district's horse-drawn vans is shown unloading the children.

by saying, "Keep going, Lady. We'll be home soon."

Lloyd pulled his collar a little closer around his head and brushed some of the snow out of his face as the blizzard seemed to be getting worse. He had no sooner made himself a bit more comfortable when Lady stopped. He looked around to see why. They were right at the door of some house. It wasn't his house, but at least he would be able to save himself from the blizzard.

What a surprise! The house turned out to be that of the Killin family, and they were just as surprised to see Lloyd as he was to see them. Lady had changed directions in

the storm, so as not to face it, and had brought him safely to the home of his friends who lived a couple of miles in the opposite direction to that of the Andersons. Lady probably reasoned that while it would be difficult to make it home against the storm, there was a better chance of making it to the neighbors' by travelling with the storm. She had been there many times before, so she knew its wherabouts.

The pioneers of the Aylesford S.D. 2836 (Maple Creek, Saskatchewan) must have planned well when Hector Russell built their school and small barn in 1909. In the fifty years that the school operated, both buildings accommodated their respective inhabitants satisfactorily, never being overcrowded, or never too thin in ranks. According to Peter Perrin who attended the school in the early days:

Not many horses were sheltered in the school barn during school hours. However, it filled to overflowing, well nigh bulging, with steaming nags when a school Christmas concert, party, or dance was in progress. In order to accommodate as many horses as possible in the limited space, the riders or drivers were instructed to do the halter shanks up and shove the animals through the door loose, in the same manner as loading a stock car. On occasions, the horses were packed so tightly that all the teamsters and riders had to decide to leave the "doings" together so when the barn door was opened, the owners of the near-at-hand horses were there to pick them up. It was impossible to do any cutting or sorting. Some of the horses had come from a considerable distance, so it was the only fair way of unscrambling them.

Getting Off Was Easy

Once a small child got off his horse, voluntarily or accidentally, the hardest task facing the tot was to climb back on, especially if he had been riding bareback and there was no saddle to use for leverage. Most parents were aware of the problem and erected small wooden platforms near the wire gates, where the children had to dismount to open them. Without such convenient pedestals the resourceful youngsters relied on the barbed wire fence, nearby boulders, a clump of shrubs, or similiar makeshift underprops.

Edna (Elkin) Raymond, who attended Grassy Lake S. D. 770 (Penhold, Alberta) in the late 1920s, remembers the novel approach her father employed to solve the problem.

I recall how dad trained our school horse Kelly to lie down for us children so we could get on and then have Kelly get up. What a help this trick turned out to be when there was no fence or saddle to aid us.

It was an accepted part of a teacher's duties to help the smaller pupils mount their horses whenever they had difficulties on their own. Rose (Cotton) Bebb, the teacher in the Sunrise S.D. 2079 (Killam, Alberta)

A shortcut through the field on the way to Hazeldean S.D. 195 (Deloraine, Manitoba).

from 1928 to 1934, remembers that such obligations were not without their interesting sidelights.

There were many occasions for me to help the children with their horses, although I must admit that my knowledge of how to handle the equine species was a poor second compared to the expertise of my lowliest grade one pupil.

One afternoon Dennis rushed back, almost distraught, to my desk and blurted out, "L-lll-leon lll-lll-losttt hh-hiss lll-lll-lidd!"

This is Ethel Haffner, the teacher of Wide Awake S.D. 2711 (Endiang, Alberta) about 1925, ready to start for her school two miles away. Donkeys were not often used for riding or driving to school, but in some rural districts they served this purpose very well, especially if their natural obstinacy was understood and could be tolerated.

This was difficult for him to say, for when he was excited he would stutter. Leon had started off for home on his horse but had lost his cap. He dared not get off to retrieve it, for he knew he could not get back on. And when Dennis tried to hand it back to him, Leon couldn't reach it and still hold onto the reins. It was a simple matter for me, with my five-foot-five height, to solve their seemingly insurmountable problem.

Every time I helped my youngsters solve such a simple dilemma or performed some menial task for them, I was always reminded of a saying that our principal at the Camrose Normal School kept repeating to us, his student teachers, "If you can't do great things in your little rural school, do the necessary small things in a great way!" I never forgot this maxim and felt heartened every time I helped any of my students over their spot of trouble, no matter how minor.

Journey by Dogsled

One of the more unusual ways of going to a prairie school was by dogsled. Walter Viste, a grade one pupil in the Wiese S.D. (Hanna, Alberta), did this for three winters, 1936-39. The Manly Viste family lived a distance of about one mile across country from the school, and Walter had no difficulty in getting there during spring, summer, or fall by walking. However, when winter set in, he travelled to and from school on a sled pulled by Buster, a large German shepherd dog.

His first trip with Buster was not only a real experience but also a very proud moment for the six-year-old boy. Mr. Viste went along to select the best trail across country, to nail up any obstructing fences, and to instruct his son on how to handle the frisky dog. The route eventually staked out was a mile and a quarter in length, and before winter was over, Walter and Buster often made the trip in six minutes.

Every trip turned out to be an adventure. Buster had a weakness for chasing rabbits, coyotes, cars, or any other moving thing that captured his fancy. When these sudden and unexpected forays occurred, Walter experienced more than his share of spills and thrills. If he fell off, Buster paid no attention whatsoever to his master, but continued the pursuit. It wasn't until the dog had satisfied his chasing urge that he would eventually stop and wait for the boy to catch up.

The incident that Walter remembered best was the time that Buster took off after three coyotes. The sudden lurch sent young Viste headlong into a snowbank. By the time he picked himself up, the dog and coyotes had disappeared over a hill. What a crucial moment for the boy! No dog, no sleigh, and only the prospect of a long walk in the blowing snow before him. He stood there and cried. The intense cold soon jarred him from this display of self-pity, and he made up his mind to head for home. Just at this moment Buster reappeared. The dog

even looked sorry as he gazed sympathetically at his tearful master. In the past, after such an escapade, the dog was punished by a good swift kick directed at the spot where the lad thought it would hurt the most. But this time he was so glad to see the German shepherd that he hugged him and patted his head. Buster accepted punishment as if he knew he deserved it. On the other hand, he spurned affection and looked bored and uncomfortable any time he was petted.

At school the dog had a "hands off" attitude as far as the other children were concerned. If anyone tried to handle him or get on the sleigh, he would growl deeply in warning; if the child persisted, Buster would put the run on him. During the day he stood tied in the school barn just like the horses. At noon he received his usual sandwich, two thick slices of bread with a slab of lard between them.

In 1936 when the first blizzard came up and caught Walter at school, the boy never had any doubts about getting home with the dog. However, the father became worried for the safety of his son and saddled a horse and rode to the Wiese School to get him. Young Viste was so confident and adamant that he could make it home by himself that he persuaded his father to let him go. Strange as it may seem, the boy and his dog arrived home a good twenty minutes ahead of their prospective rescuer. In fact, Walter was thinking of going back for his father.

The wooden runners that came with the sled didn't last too long so Roy Embree, a mechanic in Watts, designed a set of steel ones. Even at that, by the time Buster retired these had worn paper thin.

During one winter the dog pulled both Walter and his younger brother, Calton, to school daily without once being absent or

Whatever power could be spared from essential farm work was used to pull the school vehicle, even if it meant teaming a shetland pony and an old workhorse. This unlikely combination was used in Sunrise S.D. 2079 (Killam, Alberta) in 1930.

101

late. However, by spring, Walter was fed up with this arrangement as he had to kneel on the back of the sleigh behind his brother, who was comfortably seated at the front. It wasn't always easy for him to maintain his balance and stay on the sleigh in such an awkward position. Besides, the snow had built up to such an extent under the nailed-up fences that the boys, especially Walter, had to duck quickly every time they drove through these gaps. More than once they didn't react fast enough and either lost their headgear or were swept bodily into some nearby snowdrift. Buster seemed to enjoy these forays under the fences and would often speed up just to see how his young riders would fare. If dogs can have a sense of humor, Buster possessed more than his share.

After three winters Mr. Viste decided that Buster, who had served the family so faithfully, deserved a well earned rest, and the dog was relieved of his duty of pulling the sleigh. It was indeed a sad moment for the Viste household when the tried-and-true Buster was replaced by a saddle pony.[1]

Marooned

No history of the one-room prairie school would be complete without an account of how students and teacher carried on when a blizzard marooned them in their schoolhouse. One of the most tragic occurred in the Congress S.D. 3236, sixteen miles northeast of Admiral, Saskatchewan. Hilda (Wetterstrand) Watts, a participant in the drama, tells the story.

The morning of January 11, 1917, dawned mild and calm, with just enough fluffy snowflakes fluttering around to present a peaceful, Christmas card scene. My father was in a happy frame of mind that morning when he took my brother, my three sisters, and me to the Congress School. We were a jovial group in the sleigh drawn by a team of fast-stepping horses, little realizing what would happen before nightfall.

By noon a blizzard had come up. Visibility was so bad that it was impossible to see the barn from the school. The teacher, a young lady of nineteen years, had been instructed not to let the children outside in case of a bad storm. However, she consented to escort seven of us to the toilet after we had badgered her for some time. We held hands to form a protective chain, but as we raced around the northeast corner of the schoolhouse, some of us stumbled and fell into the deep drift of snow that the northwest wind had piled up. Lila (McIntyre) Magnusson, fourteen years of age, and I, thirteen at the time, managed to hold on to each other during the spill and somehow were able to reach the barn. We waited for a while for the others to appear, but when they didn't, we decided to return to the school. We managed to make it but were stunned to learn that the others had not yet come back. We all waited and hoped, but the afternoon dragged by without a sign of our teacher or any of the classmates who had ventured outside with her.

Late in the afternoon we received a most welcome but unexpected visitor, a bachelor who lived half a mile from the school. He had fastened one end of a roll of binder twine to his shack, and by playing out the cord as he went along, he was able to retain his sense of direction in the blinding blizzard and in time reach the school safely. Two of the boys attending our school stayed at his place, so he had wanted to make sure that they were safe. As the two boys were also the school janitors, he helped them bring in more coal, and at the same time tried to assure us that things would turn out all right. But for the present there was no way

1. Walter Viste, interview by his son Donald Viste for historical research essay competition, 1970.

Rural students had to be prepared to ride to school in all kinds of weather, even a snowstorm in June, 1942. Verda Oliver is riding her school horse to the Wooler S.D. (Rocky Mountain House, Alberta) through the unseasonable snow.

of finding out the whereabouts of the students and teacher who had left the school earlier in the afternoon.

The blizzard raged on relentlessly and seemed to get worse as nightfall approached. We were able to keep warm, but as there were no lamps in the school, we left the door of the stove slightly ajar, enabling the flames of the burning coal to produce a flickering, eerie glow. The young children were afraid of the strange darkness and soon began to whimper and then cry, all the while begging the older students to take them home. Eventually we arranged a number of desks near the stove and put the smaller children to bed on the seats, covering them with our coats. It was a long, agonizing night!

The teacher, Cora Hazleton, and my sister Mildred, who was eleven years of age, had found themselves together after the fall, so they linked their arms together and continued to walk in what they thought was the direction of the barn. They missed it completely and headed out onto the open prairie. They tramped through the drifting snow for over a mile with their coat sleeves frozen together. The teacher became exhausted and wanted to sit down in the snow and rest, but Mildred, realizing how hazardous this would be, kept pulling her along.

Eventually, they bumped into what seemed to be a wooden fence, but when they followed it, they discovered that it was a wall of a building of some sort. Soon they located a place where a strip of canvas had been hung over a door to keep out the wind. When they tried to fling the canvas cover aside, the family inside the homesteader's shack heard the rustling sound and opened the door. The two girls tumbled into the house and fell on the floor, completely exhausted. My sister did not fare too badly, suffering only from a few frost blisters on her wrists where her mitts did not reach the sleeves of her coat. The teacher, on the other hand, was exhausted from shock as well as experiencing agonizing pains from her badly frozen hands and feet. Fortunately, she eventually made a complete recovery.

Marguerite, thirteen; Hortense, twelve; and Corinne, eleven; the three daughters of Mr. and Mrs. O. Z. Dechamp; and my sister Esther, nine years of age, were able to hold fast to one another after falling down in the huge snowdrift. Unfortunately, they lost their sense of direction in the blinding

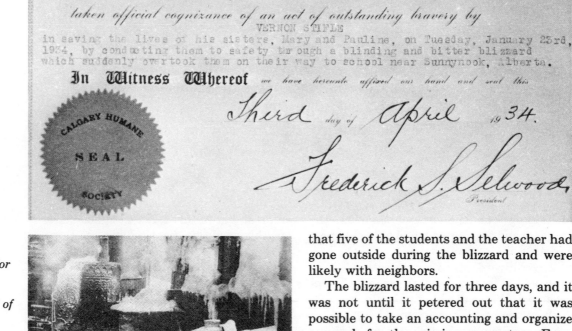

This Certificate of Merit was presented to student Vernon Stifle of Sunnynook S.D. 4788 for saving the lives of his two sisters by conducting them safely through a blinding prairie blizzard on January 23, 1934.

CALGARY HUMANE SOCIETY

Certificate of Merit

This Is To Certify *that the Calgary Humane Society has taken official cognizance of an act of outstanding bravery by*

VERNON STIFLE

in saving the lives of his sisters, Mary and Pauline, on Tuesday, January 23rd, 1934, by conducting them to safety through a blinding and bitter blizzard which suddenly overtook them on their way to school near Sunnynook, Alberta.

In Witness Whereof *we have hereunto affixed our hand and seal this*

Third day of April 19 34.

Frederick S. Selwood,
President

CALGARY HUMANE SEAL SOCIETY

A picture of the interior of McCann S.D. 2562 the morning after the fierce March blizzard of 1938. Snow drove through the cracks in the walls and a broken window to pile drifts right up to window sills and fill the attic, and the space between the stove jacket and the stove itself was packed solidly. It took Frank Jacobs, the teacher, a whole day to shovel it out of the schoolhouse. As the snow above the ceiling began to melt, water dripped on everything. Fortunately, on the day of the blizzard the teacher kept nine children overnight after notifying their parents by fence-line phone that all were safe.

blizzard and drifted aimlessly with the wind at their backs. They were found huddled together, frozen to death, in a coulee half a mile from the school. Marguerite, with her back to the wind, had her arms clasped around the other three, as if to protect them from the fury of the blizzard.

We remained marooned in the schoolhouse until the next afternoon, when my father somehow managed to reach us in the howling blizzard. He took all the children that were left to our home, where they stayed that night. I shall never forget the look on my father's face when I told him

that five of the students and the teacher had gone outside during the blizzard and were likely with neighbors.

The blizzard lasted for three days, and it was not until it petered out that it was possible to take an accounting and organize a search for the missing youngsters. Even their discovery turned out to be tragic, for it was the two fathers most deeply concerned in the quest who first came across the ghastly scene of the four frozen bodies of their daughters.

Congress School was built in 1915 and was in reality a summer school. The school terms usually started on the first of April and ended just before Christmas; 1917 was the only year that they attempted to hold a winter school.

The Congress School was closed years ago and has since been sold and moved away from its original site. If any good can come out of such a tragedy, it could be that it lent strength to the movement across the country to have every school yard fenced and a telephone installed in each school where possible.

Chapter Seven

Special Days

The School Fair

In the era of the one-room schoolhouse, one of the most important events of the year was the school fair. Since the number of rural schools included in a fair center had to be sufficient to justify the expense of the event, eight was considered a minimum and twenty-five a maximum. The fair was a one-day occasion held between August 25 and October 9 at a central location. There were competitive classes in livestock, cooking, sewing, knitting, garden produce, and all phases of schoolwork. Frequently a picnic and a program of sports were held in conjunction with the fair.

Preparation for the fair almost approached a fever pitch. In the Stockland S.D. (Midnapore, Alberta), even a lad who didn't like school or anything connected with it was affected.

Jim McNab just couldn't get used to the confinement dictated by a classroom. Yet once during the eight years he attended school, Jim did put his heart into doing something that won a teacher's approval: the school fair.

The new school fair booklet had just been received by the teacher and she brought it to school to show the pupils. Actually it wasn't really new, for it contained the same classes of competition that had been used for years and years. The date on the cover was the only apparent change; it now read 1926 instead of 1925.

Since the students appeared interested, the teacher started to read the objectives of a school fair to them: "1. To stimulate in the children an interest in the activities of the farm, the home, and the school. 2. To increase their knowledge of the principles and practices of farming and homemaking." She droned on, "3. To encourage the teaching of agri- . . . . James McNab, if all you can

"On your marks! Get ready! Set! Go!" The end-of-school picnic was one of the most anticipated events of the year and always ran the Christmas concert a close second. Nothing, not even a black eye, neckties, shoes, overalls, giant hair ribbons, good Sunday clothes, tight skirt, or a poor track, prevented the enthusiastic children of St. George S.D. 3226 (Watts, Alberta) from participating in each and every event at their 1925 school picnic.

The annual school picnics were always fun, and the peanut scramble, like this one at Sheerness S.D. 2214 (Sheerness, Alberta) in late June, 1939, added to the excitement of the day.

do is sit there and make fun of my accent, you can just get outside!"

This teacher had just arrived at the Stockland School two weeks ago, and Jim was provoking her already. He never did hear the rest of the objectives of a school fair.

During the afternoon recess the girls were teasing Jim about what he was going to enter in the fair.

"How about your geography notebook?" someone suggested.

All the girls started to giggle at this loaded question, because just yesterday, Jim

A typical scene at a school fair, judging calves. Five rural schools — Brampton, Asceola, Green Prairie, Rolling Prairie, and the host school, Robin Hood — brought their exhibits in 1920. All these school districts are located near the city of Moose Jaw, Saskatchewan.

Roy Lobb, one of the exhibitors in the school section of the poultry class, proudly displays his leghorn entry at the Gladstone Fair in Gladstone, Manitoba, in 1916.

had stood up and ripped it in half when the teacher had told him it was "too messy." What was left of it had been used to light the fire that very morning.

There and then, Jim decided he would get even with these meddlesome, snickering girls. He was going to enter the "Apple Pie — Two Crusts" competition, the class that every girl from every school entered in the fair would like to win.

Jim was living with his grandparents at the time, so when he got home that afternoon, he immediately asked his grandmother's permission to enter the pie-baking competition. She nodded her approval, a bit pessimistically, and when baking day arrived she was more pessimistic than ever.

"Jimmy, did you wash your hands?" she inquired.

"What for?" he innocently asked.

"Jimmy, you've been out helping Dave with the chores all morning. You mean to tell me that after milking cows and feeding pigs, you're going to dive right into making a pie?"

Jim knew better than to argue with his grandmother, so he went to the pump and gave his hands a good scrubbing.

The moment of truth had arrived! Jim rolled up his sleeves, measured the ingredients with less than perfect accuracy, and mixed them all together. Lo and behold, it was beginning to look like pastry already. He divided the dough into two balls, handling them more like a couple of snowballs than like flaky pie pastry. He slammed them on the cake board and went to work on them with the rolling pin. What was on Jim's mind no one will ever know, but the pastry received a terrific pummelling.

"Don't work it so hard, Jim! You're not chopping wood," his grandmother warned.

Eventually the pie shell was finished, and Jim set to work to prepare the filling. Luckily, he had skinned more than his share of rabbits and coyotes, and peeling apples wasn't too different. But he did admit afterwards that he would have preferred stripping a coyote as he couldn't get used to the dinky paring knife.

The school fair in the hall at Leo, Alberta, in 1919.

The preparation of the apples for the filling was the most demanding part of pie making, and Jim followed the recipe in the instruction pamphlet as closely as possible. The only part of the whole process that he enjoyed was stretching the pastry over the top, sealing and fluting the edges, and pricking the upper crust in five or six places with a fork. At last his artwork was finished and the pie was ready for the hot oven in the wood-burning stove.

Jim's grandmother had never known him to be so excited and particular as he anxiously watched the oven thermometer and the kitchen clock while his pie was baking. When the time was up, Jim quickly opened the oven door and was beside himself with joy when he saw how delicious his pie looked.

The Red Deer Lake Hall and grounds were a scene of much activity and excitement on the morning of the day of the school fair. Democrats, buggies, wagons, and Model T automobiles were arriving from all directions. Mothers were busily helping their children carry in the exhibits, while the fathers were unharnessing the teams and finding suitable places to tether them. Youngsters flooded the grounds as they raced around exuberantly. In the hall, the fair officials were accepting the tagged exhibits and arranging them on the various tables according to their respective classes and age groups. The instant the deadline for receiving the entries was reached, a gong sounded. The officials shooed everyone out of the hall and closed the doors, and the judging began.

Meanwhile, the sports events were getting underway on the specially prepared ground north of the hall. The shouts and gleeful screams of the children could be heard everywhere as they participated in the various events or cheered for their classmates and school. The adults stood around in groups chatting with their friends and neighbors, as well as taking a casual interest in the proceedings on the sports grounds. Little children ran around playing tag and hide and go seek or just romping around in the excitement of the moment. At noon the women set out a picnic lunch and for the first time in the day, the good food and the hot sun gently quieted the crowd.

After the lunch the doors of the hall were opened and the crowd immediately surged in that direction. The children rushed ahead, dashed up the steps, and quickly disappeared into the building. The parents followed more sedately.

Jim had been busy doing something else, so it wasn't until later that he remembered the exhibits in the hall. When he arrived, he noticed that a large crowd had gathered around the table that displayed the baking entries. He pushed his way forward and soon saw what everyone was looking at: a first-prize red ribbon clipped to the entry tag on his apple pie. A boy, a boy who had never made an apple pie before in his life, had triumphed over the best cooks from eight schools.[1]

Travelling Clinics

Crop failure was a way of life for the people who settled in the Chinook district of southeastern Alberta between 1911 and 1940. On the average the farmers in the area harvested one good crop every four years and had to be content with meager returns for the remaining three years of the cycle. The lack of money in almost every home in the district resulted in hardships of all kinds, since only the essentials could be provided. Medical treatment, which should have been one of the first priorities for both children and adults, had to be passed up, not only because there just wasn't the money to pay

1. James McNab, interview by Elaine Taylor for historical research essay competition, 1970.

for it, but also because capable doctors were few and far between in the newly settled, impoverished area.

The government of the United Farmers of Alberta that was in power at the time immediately became sympathetic to the farmers' plight. The Honorable George Hoadley, the minister of health and welfare, and Dr. Roy Washburn, the superintendent of the University Hospital in Edmonton, came up with the idea of a travelling medical clinic that would visit the economically depressed areas of the province. The clinic was equipped to provide medical examinations; perform minor operations, especially the removal of diseased tonsils and adenoids; make dental examinations; put in fillings; and extract troublesome teeth. A government report issued in 1929 on the work of the clinic during that summer indicates something of the extent and nature of its services.

Since May 27, 1929, forty-one communities have been given relief: 4,413 examinations were made by Dr. R. T. Washburn, the superintendent of the University Hospital and head of the clinic, who performed 1,408 tonsil and adenoid operations, 147 minor operations, and 93 circumcisions. In this work he had the assistance of Dr. Margaret Owen. In all, 1,689 anaesthetics, including 168 for teeth alone, were given by Dr. Owen.

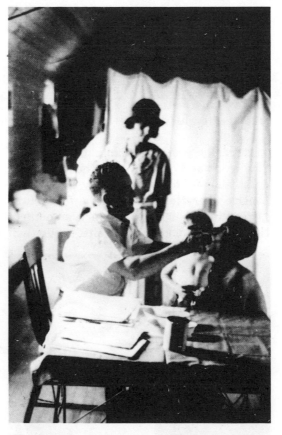

Dr. Gilchrist examining teeth during the visit of the mobile clinic to the Peace River area of Alberta in 1939. The dentist is checking the teeth of two boys while the mother watches.

The dental section was equally busy, for Dr. Haycock, government dentist, and Dr. H. A. Gilchrist of the University of Alberta made 4,273 dental examinations, put in 1,150 fillings, and extracted 2,775 teeth. The nursing staff including the misses Olive

Everyone, including public health nurses, used whatever mode of transportation was available to get to isolated schools. Here Mrs. F. Anderson at Norway House, Manitoba, in 1941 is preparing to embark by dog team to reach some of the rural schools in the outlying areas.

Watherson, Agnes McLeod, E. M. Davidson, and Anna Young rendered valiant support to the doctors and dentists.[2]

Norman D. Stewart, a 1920 pioneer of the Collhome S.D. 2752 (Chinook, Alberta) recalls vividly the time in 1931 when the tonsil clinic visited his school.

It really was something to remember! The truck and cars carrying the equipment and the clinic staff arrived early, and by nine o'clock everything was ready for action. Depending upon their itinerary, sometimes the clinic arrived the day before, set up their

Nurse E. Davidson, a member of the travelling medical clinic, outside of the operating tent at Oyen, Alberta, in June, 1930.

tents for accommodation, and camped overnight in the school yard. It always reminded me of the arrival of a circus. Usually the children flooded in from all directions and distances, even before the clinic was ready for them. I know of one family who came over twenty-five miles to have their children attended to. They came over to our house

after their operations to rest and recuperate, and to try to eat some supper.

Twelve feet at the front of the Collholme School was curtained off to become not only the operating room for the doctors but also the locale of the gruesome-looking dental chair for those requiring fillings or extractions. There was no electricity available so the doctors and dentists relied on the good prairie sunshine for light by which to operate. All the desks in the school were taken outside and replaced with so many cots that there was barely room to get between them. Some of these cots had been brought by the clinic but the majority were supplied by the local people. Eaton's of Winnipeg must have done a good sales job in our district for almost every cot carried the Eaton's trademark on it.

When the children came out of the "operating room," they were placed on these cots, the majority of them crying bitterly more from fright than from pain. Nevertheless, they were poor company for the youngsters on the adjoining cots who were awaiting their turn to go in. The dentists turned out their share of screaming, crying kids too so all in all, the Collhome School sounded like a very unhappy nursery. Every human sound indicative of fear or pain was heard at one time or another during that hectic day.

The clinic staff worked until noon, when they took a couple of hours off to clean up, have lunch, and prepare for the afternoon session.

The school had been asked to provide a couple of chore boys, so Wilfred Morrison and Ewart Duncan, who had volunteered for the job, were kept busy most of the day doing simple but unique tasks. They carried water from Horace Dunster's farm twenty rods away and emptied the slop pails of blood-tinged water with floating tonsils. The refuse provided a good meal for the gophers that were acting as observers. Two local nurses, my wife and Jessie Morrison, provided assistance in handling the patients

2. The Honorable George Hoadley, Minister of Health and Welfare, in a report presented to the Fall Session of the Alberta Legislature, 1929.

Health inspection of a school child by a public health nurse in 1923, Brookland, Manitoba.

before and after their operations. My wife also looked after two families of parents and children who came to our house a mile away when they felt like being moved. Supper was served to those who were able to eat.

Children were not the only ones who received treatment at this clinic, for many adults took advantage of the opportunity to get medical attention that they could not otherwise have afforded. I'm not certain about the cost, but I believe it was three dollars for a tonsil operation. However, if the patient was not able to pay, the fee was waived. I remember Bill Shier, who was forty years old at the time, had his tonsils removed and was really sick afterwards. A bad reaction was common in the case of adults. By half-past five the clinic staff had finished their operations and moved out. Poor Bill was left all alone in the schoolhouse, as his wife and family were at our place. We went to get him at six o'clock and found him very dejected and glum, but noticeably glad to see us arrive. He was

elated to get back to his wife and family, but eating was still out of the question.

I'm told that if a tonsillectomy is improperly done, there is a real danger of the tonsils growing back again, but of all the patients who went through that tonsil clinic in the Collhome School, I have never heard of one who had any future trouble. The majority of the children and adults who attended the clinic would not otherwise have had service from any doctor.

The clinic was valuable for another reason. The doctor often found some minor defect in a child of which the parents were unaware. The condition was corrected rather than allowed to persist until it became serious. As a result of such an experience, the parents thought of themselves and decided that a general checkup of their own and their other children would be advantageous. Relief from suffering, expert medical advice, and greater interest in health matters followed the visit of the clinic to Collhome School in 1931.

Box Socials

The Dunlop S.D. 2150 (Jackfish Lake, Manitoba), like many other rural schools, sponsored box socials to raise money to buy much needed library books, the odd ball or bat, gifts for the children at Christmas time, or anything else that was needed but which the school board could not afford to provide. So when Eva Mills, an eighteen-year-old schoolmarm, first came to the district in 1933, she took more than a passing interest in these box socials. They had a special appeal for her, and today she is able to recapture a good deal of the atmosphere that usually surrounded such affairs.

As the people approached the log schoolhouse, they invariably heard the music of a scratchy fiddle and perhaps the thump of a guitar. The small interior of the building would be packed with humanity, and there would always be the roaring stove greedily consuming cordwood and roasting everyone venturing near it. Then at the appointed time, the fiddler stopped, and Oscar Hart patiently and good naturedly cleared the floor for the auction sale of the boxes. The ladies had brought along beautifully decorated boxes in the shapes of wagons, horses, barns, or even shoes, each containing a fancy lunch. It was understood that the successful bidder got to eat the lunch with the owner of the box. Of course, the buyer didn't know whose it was until he opened it. Good-natured bantering and bidding with Mr. Hart acting as the auctioneer continued until the last box was sold.

I always found it intriguing just to pause and survey the scene in the classroom, especially taking note of the people who were sitting and watching the auction or the dance. The school benches had been arranged along the four walls, with those at the back of the room reserved for the babies. There they slept soundly on piles of coats, oblivious to the heat, dust, and noise. Against the right wall sat the mothers, the daughters, the child-wives, the spinsters, an eighteen-year-old girl nursing her third baby, and a woman of forty holding her fourteenth child. Across from them sat those of the opposite sex who didn't dance. They were silent and impassive, only their eyes taking in everything with a knowing glance.

The box social had many variations: the pie social, at which pies were auctioned along with a package of sandwiches; the tie social, at which lunch was supplied by the lady who wore the apron matching the tie sold by the auctioneer; or the shadow social, where from behind a sheet in a dark room, Mr. Hart auctioned each lady's shadow and the special lunch she had prepared.

Sponsoring a box social and dance had many other implications. Margaret Wood of the Grenville S.D. 3259 (Sibbald, Alberta) remembers that it was the custom for everyone to bring sandwiches and either cake or cookies to school functions. It was taken for granted that at your own school you brought both to make up for the bachelors, who were not expected to bring any lunch. Of course, there was always the problem of the people who made excuses for not bringing any or for bringing very little lunch: the angel food cake that fell as it was removed from the oven, the unexpected company, the hungry schoolchildren who made short work of the special cookies that had just been baked. Many times these were the very people who attended the majority of the dances held in the surrounding rural schools, so they became well known for their less than munificent lunch offerings.

At one pie social held at Grenville School, a fellow succeeded in buying a pie, but the woman refused to eat with him. He just tossed it calmly into a corner, saying loudly enough for everyone in the school to hear, "If it isn't good enough for you, it isn't good enough for me!"

It was also the practice in the district for the women to make four or five pies and bring them to the school to sell. The names of the women who hadn't brought any were often generously affixed to these extras, making the bidding uncertain but interesting. At one social, Mabel, one of the best cooks in the district, had brought some extra pies along and labelled them with the names of other women. Her husband happened to be the successful bidder on one of these pies, and, of course, had lunch with the other woman. After lunch he kept raving to his wife about the wonderful pie the other woman had made. He even suggested to her that she try to get the recipe!

At the next school "do" that same husband was looking for his wife's pie with more than his usual determination. He kept repeating that he would never hear the end of it if he didn't get Mabel's pie, no matter what he had to pay for it. Bidding at pie socials in this district was keenly competitive, so if a fellow wanted to get his girl's or wife's pie, he was often forced to pay a handsome price for it. This was due in part to a knot of bachelors, who in the earlier days attended every dance anywhere around and had some fun at the expense of the local people. If a fellow wanted a pie badly enough, the bachelors bid it out of all proportion. Thus it was that the unfortunate husband not only was forced to pay an exorbitant price for his wife's pie, but also incurred her ire for being "stupid" enough to spend so much money for it. She could have easily baked five pies for him at home for that amount.

Saint Valentine's Day

Normal schools advised their student teachers not to disrupt the regular work of the school unduly in celebrating Saint Valentine's Day. Yet in the same breath they recommended, "A little nonsense now and then is relished by the best of men and presumably will not do harm to school children." So most teachers put on valentine parties.

On the day itself a valentine box was placed on the teacher's desk to receive the valentines. The students were encouraged to send one to all their school friends so none would be disappointed. The box, usually an old shoe box, was appropriately decorated for the occasion with hearts, cupids, flowers and doilies, and a letter slot cut in the top. At the end of the party a couple of pupils carried the love missives to those for whom they were intended. These bearers had a large red heart made of cardboard suspended around their necks with a string.

There were very few store-bought valentines in the early days of the rural school as the children made their own. The days before the Saint Valentine's party became a round of folding, cutting, gluing, drawing, lettering, and coloring. For the most part, valentines were made from sheets of paper from writing tablets scrounged from home. The teacher supplied the bits of red, blue, silver, or gold paper with which to trim them. Catalogues, wallpaper sample books, and advertising folders, if available, were also used. Some valentines turned out to be works of art trimmed with paper lace, cupids, doves, flowers, and arrows; others, the work of the grade ones or the lackadaisical older boys, consisted of misshapen hearts bearing the words, "Be My Valentine" crudely scrawled in colored crayon. The two or three store-bought valentines that appeared in the box were destined for the teacher or for the "one and only."

Another reason why all the students looked forward to the party was the special goodies that the teacher provided for them. Since most teacherages were not equipped with any type of refrigeration, the treats were buried in a snowdrift to keep them fresh. Although the children knew about the presence of these luxuries in the school yard, they never dared to touch them. They respected their teacher too much to indulge in any unscrupulous activity.

Wandering animals, however, were not so prudish. Pigs, coyotes, skunks, badgers, dogs, horses, or cattle must have had a sweet tooth, for they enjoyed the teacher's treats as much as the children did if they got to them before the party was underway. Their keen sense of smell often led them directly to the cache, and by the time anyone was aware of what was happening, not many of the goodies were left.

To the children attending Balmoral S.D. 292 (Red Deer, Alberta) in the mid-1920s it wasn't the loss of their treats to a pack of coyotes that created the excitement on Saint Valentine's Day. It was cupid himself! The teacher that year was a very attractive widow who was creating quite a stir among the bachelors of the district and the nearby town. About midmorning one of the local swains arrived at the school with chocolates for the teacher. She tried unsuccessfully to spirit the heart-shaped box into one of the school cupboards without the children seeing it. To make matters worse, before the gift bearer had left the school yard, another suitor arrived from town, also carrying a heart-shaped box of chocolates for the teacher. The scuffle that ensued in the school yard was magnified in the imaginations of the pupils by the fact that they didn't dare leave their seats to watch it.

"What a fight!" was the only comment that the residents of the district heard from the pupils.[3]

The Christmas Concert

There was no doubt in the mind of Rose (Cotton) Bebb that her first Christmas concert in the Selby S.D. 1454 (Killam, Alberta) in 1915 was a learning experience.

As in all country schools, our learning experiences went far beyond the three Rs and the classroom. However, for me, the real learning experience came when the teacher arranged to have a Christmas concert. The program would be made up of songs, drills, dialogues, and recitations. Well do I remember the Japanese drill we executed, running in short steps and waving small paper fans in unison. My brother's first experience in reciting occurred before he was of school age, when he stood on a chair to open the concert with "The Welcome Speech."

I am but a tiny tot
And I haven't much to say
But, I must make, I'm told
The welcome speech today.

Dear friends: We're glad you've come
To hear us speak and sing.
We'll do our very best
To please in everything.

Our speeches we have learned,
And, if you'll hear us through,
You'll see what little folk
If they but try, can do.[4]

3. Esme James, account of Balmoral S.D. 292, in *Mingling Memories*, Red Deer East Historical Society (Calgary: Friesen Printers, 1979), 47.

4. Rose (Cotton) Bebb describing her experiences in four Alberta country schools, 1914. At Selby S.D. 1545 (Killam, Alberta) Mary Macdonald, the teacher who boarded at the Cotton home, taught William Thomas Cotton this recitation, which she had made up.

Christmas songs, apart from the familiar carols, were sung to the tunes that were popular at the time. The old song book entitled *Heart Songs,* which was in many homes, was always in evidence whenever there was a musical event in the school. However, the most welcome musical sound of all was heard at the end of the program when Santa Claus entered, ringing a string of sleigh bells.

One year we did not have the usual type of concert. Our teacher provided entertainment by showing lantern slides and narrating the story of *A Christmas Carol.* We were not thrilled and as youngsters voiced our disapproval by our own program of passive resistance. Our teacher got the message, for next Christmas we put on our customary concert.

Eaton's Christmas Tree Shopping Service

Pioneer rural schoolteachers were of the opinion that The T. Eaton Co. Limited of Winnipeg was the *real* Santa Claus when it came time to make plans for the annual Christmas concert and tree. The special mail-order Christmas Tree Shopping Service that Eaton's offered to schools could only be described as magnanimous.

Early in September every school district in Canada received a Christmassy-looking green order form. All the busy schoolteacher had to do was to write in the ages and number of boys and girls for whom presents were needed, enclose the amount of money collected in the district for the Christmas expenses, and make sure to indicate the date of the concert.

The Eaton's Christmas Tree Shopping Service did the rest. They gift wrapped the presents, labelled them as to age and boy/girl suitability, and sent the parcel in plenty of time to reach its destination by the date indicated on the order form. It was a simple matter for the teacher to write the name of the appropriate pupil on the Christmas tag attached to each gift package and then place them all under the school Christmas tree. Santa Claus did the rest.

Rita Desilets wore a glamorous rainbow crepe paper dress in her role as mistress of ceremonies at the 1930 Christmas concert in Corinth S.D. 2924 (Sunnynook, Alberta). But it wasn't until months later that a camera was available to record the event. In the meantime, Rita had grown at least an additional couple of inches.

One of the keys to the success of this Christmas Tree Shopping Service was the well devised order form. It was easy to fill out and invited the teacher to participate in the gift selections. Judging from the instruc-

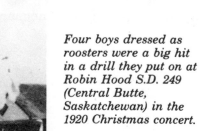

Four boys dressed as roosters were a big hit in a drill they put on at Robin Hood S.D. 249 (Central Butte, Saskatchewan) in the 1920 Christmas concert.

EATON'S
Mail Order
Christmas Tree
Shopping Service

This **EATON** Service offers a simple and easy plan for the handling of bulk orders of prizes, toys, novelties, etc. It is maintained to assist Institutions, Societies, Schools and other groups who have the pleasant duty of distributing large numbers of gifts at Christmas time.

NOW . . . While Our Stocks are Most Complete
is the Time to Send in Your Orders.
LET US . . . Make Your Gift Selections!

Looking through our Fall and Winter Catalogue, you will find that many items are splendid for Christmas gifts. We will make up your order with suitable items when merchandise you desire is not available.

Simply tell us the ages and number of boys and girls you are providing for. Enclose with the list the amount of money you wish to spend, also the date you require them and we will choose suitable gifts. Parcels will be shipped in time for your entertainment.

Below is a list of typical items. We suggest that the average cost should not be less than the prices shown. By allowing a larger amount you can be sure of a much better selection.

Kindly put an X beside class of goods desired.

		Fall and Winter Catalogue Pages
Toys	25c, 35c and up, charges extra	220, 316, 416, 417, 525-546
Books	25c and up, charges extra	416, 417, 419, 425-428
Games	25c, 35c and up, charges extra	316, 417, 419, 534-537
Combs	25c and up, price del.	218, 314, 317, 318, 325, 361, 367, 371, 373
Handkerchiefs	25c and up, price delivered	100, 101, 318
Gloves and Mitts	39c, 45c, 59c and up, price delivered	112-115, 119-122, 216, 219
Ties	29c, 35c, 50c and up, price delivered	100, 195, 283-285
Purses	45c, 59c and up, price delivered	385, 388, 389, 392
Stockings	39c, 49c, 55c and up, price del.	105-112, 116-118, 196, 215, 218, 557

See also pages 415 to 419, inclusive, and pages 548 to 557, inclusive.

Presents for older people should be separately selected from our General Catalogue if possible, using separate Order Form enclosed. When ordering, please use the reverse side of this letter; envelope is herewith enclosed. By using these they will bring your order direct to the Christmas Tree Shopping Service. Orders will be ready for shipping in time for your entertainment if you tell us the date required.

THE **T. EATON C**O LIMITED

Christmas Tree Shopping Service

If you have changed your address since your last order, please give former address | State Post Office you wish your next Catalogue sent to

THE T. EATON C⁰ LIMITED
WINNIPEG   CANADA

Mr., Mrs. or Miss   First Name   Last Name

Name in Full of Person Ordering ....

(Please Print or Letter Name and Address)

Mr., Mrs. or Miss   First Name   Last Name

Name of Head of Institution or Organization ....

To Ensure Your Receiving a Copy of the Next Catalogue, Please Give Full Name of the Head of Household.

Street Address or Box Number .... R.R. Number ....

Post Office .... Prov. ....

Your Railway Station is .... Railway ....

Ship Order by .... **Is there an agent at your station?** .... **How many miles do you live from station?** ....

STATE AMOUNT ENCLOSED

D. A. If you have a Deposit Account (D.A.) give number and Branch where account is located when ordering.

D.A. Account Number .... Located in EATON'S Branch at .... (State City)

Please Note—If you are ordering merchandise on which we do not pay charges (such as Games or Toys) to be sent by mail to your P.O. or if there is no agent at your station **Be Sure To Include Enough Money** with your order to pay the charges on these goods, otherwise we may have to omit some items.

Kindly advise us if assorted presents are required for each group or if a similar present would do for each child. Also if wearing apparel is preferred to toys.

State number of boys and girls in ages, also the amount of money you wish to spend for **each group**.

Number Infants to 2 years ....

Boys		Number	Amount Allowed	Girls		Number	Amount Allowed
2 to 4 years		....	....	2 to 4 years		....	....
" 4 to 6 years		....	....	" 4 to 6 years		....	....
" 6 to 8 years		....	....	" 6 to 8 years		....	....
" 8 to 10 years		....	....	" 8 to 10 years		....	....
" 10 to 12 years		....	....	" 10 to 12 years		....	....
" 12 to 14 years		....	....	" 12 to 14 years		....	....
" 14 years and over		....	....	" 14 years and over		....	....

Money allowed for ship. chgs. ....   Date of Entertainment ....

Please Note—It may be necessary to send your order express if we find you have not allowed sufficient time to have it go by freight.

Christmas Decorations, see pages 424, 542, 543, Fall and Winter Catalogue. Musical Novelties, page 440.

Kindly remember that if a good variety is required you should allow at least 25c to 50c per child.

23293—16-6-49—10m—167

tions given on the order form, Eaton's was most eager to provide the best gifts and services possible for the money available. At times, especially during the depression years, the amount that the teacher was able to send seemed inadequate relative to the number of gifts required and the ages of the pupils. What could Eaton's supply at five to fifteen cents per child? Yet thanks to the understanding firm, the order was filled beyond anyone's expectations. The miracle of Christmas spread from a large warehouse in Winnipeg to hundreds of tots attending small rural schools across Canada.

Many a teacher received the surprise of her life when, upon opening the school's parcel from Eaton's, she found a special treat for her students — a bag of candy. It was unbelievable! It was incredible! Yes, it was a Christmas miracle! The teacher knew very well that these sweets would be the only ones her pupils would receive for Christmas. The two or three tears that the young teacher brushed from her brimming eyes and the "thank you" she whispered under her breath were never seen or heard by Eaton's, but it is gestures like these that sing on in the soul forever. The men and women who manned the order desks in Winnipeg must have taken a deep personal pride in what they were doing to achieve such humanitarian results.

Fire!

Prior to the time of rural electrification, the lighting of the school Christmas tree for the annual concert was done by candles. These candles were about six inches in length and came in red, green, pink, blue, or white; thus, in themselves, they added grandeur to the tree. They were inserted in little tin holders and then clamped strategically on the boughs of the tree. There was an art to placement as each candle had to be set upright and positioned so it would not ignite anything above it. As the candles were lighted by matches, there was always the danger of setting fire to the tindery pine needles. As well, the trees were decorated with such homemade ornaments as strung popcorn and cranberries, paper garlands

fashioned from the colored pages of catalogues, or colored popcorn balls. All these were highly inflammable too. A pail of water and a container of sand were kept near the tree as precautionary measures, while one or two responsible individuals kept a watchful eye on the tree throughout the evening.

When one considers the burning candles, the inflammable decorations, the tissue paper costumes, and the nonfireproof stage properties, it is a miracle that more fires did not occur during these annual rural school Christmas concerts. However, it seems that many school districts experienced some kind of a fire during the Christmas concert, sufficiently dramatic about which to reminisce years thereafter.

Byron Moore, the teacher in the Annasheim S.D. 3047 (seven miles north of Craigmyle, Alberta), had reason enough to remember the concluding number on his Christmas program in 1943. It goes without saying that so did his pupils, not to mention the large crowd that had packed the schoolhouse right to its one and only doorway. Mr. Moore and his enterprising students had planned to terminate the program with an act that they thought would leave their audience spellbound. They succeeded, but not in the way they had intended.

The all-star number was a range scene with cowboys gathered around a prairie camp fire singing Christmas carols. The presentation called for a bit of ingenuity, so it was decided that the youngster tending the campfire would use the large ash pan from the school's Waterman-Waterbury heater in which to build the fire. In one corner he had a fire going, and diagonally across from it was a supply of oil-soaked rags with which to keep the flames blazing brightly. Sticks had been skillfully stacked in and around the metal pan to convey to the audience the impression that it was the wood burning, not the saturated rags.

The play proceeded with convincing reality; the boys had bacon frying and coffee boiling over their campfire, and soon such a pleasant odor filled the room that many a mouth in the audience began to water. When the boys were singing their final song,

"I'm Dreaming of a White Christmas," the flames suddenly leaped across the ash pan, ignited the oil rags and the pile of tinder-dry kindling wood. In seconds a serious fire was blazing, and it looked as if the entire schoolhouse was in danger of going up in flames. Most people stood up, while others were gradually inching their way toward the one and only exit. It was just at this moment that one of the boys, exercising great presence of mind, emptied the coffee on the fire, not only extinguishing the fire, but also ending the play and concert. A pall of smoke was still hanging over the classroom half an hour later when Santa Claus made his cheery entrance. Everyone, including Santa Claus, agreed that it was quite a night!

We'll never let the old flag fall

During the years of the First World War, the Christmas theme for most school concerts was interwoven with a patriotic one befitting a nation in a life-and-death struggle in Europe.

The Eagle S.D. 1637 (Airdrie, Alberta) was no exception. In one special number all the students, carrying Union Jack flags, marched onto the stage very smartly, then lined up in rows as if getting ready for a military inspection. The moment this maneuver was completed, they sang with an enthusiasm that only children can muster when they feel their patriotic fervor is rubbing off on their elders in the ecstatic audience. At this very climactic moment, disaster struck. Ada Ryan, a pupil participating in the patriotic display, remembers the incident vividly.

One small boy dropped his flag during the grand finale when we were supposed to wave them vigorously and sing, with all the patriotic ardor we could muster, "We'll Never Let the Old Flag Fall." What a letdown! It looked like a stain on our

Patriotism was an integral part of the program in the early schools with demonstrations, drills, and much flag waving on special occasions. In 1920 the children of Endiang S.D. 2253 (Endiang, Alberta) entertained their parents and visitors with a spectacular patriotic drill. They performed on the grounds near the United Farmers of Alberta Hall as their schoolhouse had burned in 1919.

Jewel, the homemade mule, is going through his paces just prior to the 1934 Christmas concert in Garden Plain S.D. 2941 (Hanna, Alberta). Harold and Louis, a couple of grade ones, are giving the strange saddle a good tryout.

patriotism. Imagine telling everyone that we would never let the old flag fall and having a member of our class do the very opposite. It was unforgivable!

I tried desperately to make up for this botched performance in my recitation later in the program. It was selected from *The Calgary Herald* and was all about horses and their part in the war, a very sad oration to be sure. When I received thunderous applause, I felt I had redeemed the school's patriotism, at least a little.

The finishing touch

The days of the one-room rural school could also be called the days of crepe paper. This paper with the crinkled texture came in all colors and was ideal for decorating the schoolhouse or making costumes for any special occasion, particularly the annual Christmas concert. What made it so ver-

satile was it could be stretched without tearing easily. It could be sewn, glued, pinned, pleated, flounced, fluffed, braided, trimmed, and treated dozens of other ways in the hands of a talented seamstress. Instruction books on using it, as well as a variety of patterns, were available.

No matter whether a teacher wanted to make gowns for the Alice Blue Gown drill, a costume for the girl playing the part of Little Red Riding Hood, bonnets for the senior girls in the sunbonnet choir, uniforms for the soldiers or policemen, curtains for the windows, a backdrop for the stage, pyjamas for the clowns, black habits for the witches, dresses for the girls dancing the Virginia reel, or black masks for the minstrel show, all could be made from the crepe paper. There was no limit to what could be done with the versatile paper and a little ingenuity.

Sir Roger de Coverley was an English country dance performed in two straight lines by an indefinite number of performers. It was very difficult to put on at a rural school Christmas concert as it necessitated such unusual and elaborate attire. However, costuming problems didn't deter the teacher and students of Morrin S.D. 2513 (Morrin, Alberta) from putting on a dance at their Christmas concert in 1945.

Another popular Christmas concert item was the acrostic act, as it involved as many students as the teacher desired and no youngster was ever overworked. The youngsters of Bison S.D. 2824 (Chinook, Alberta) have come up on the stage and given their individual recitations in the right order, and now proudly display the results of their efforts.

Unfortunately, crepe paper had two disadvantages. It was not fireproof in those days. Worse, being resilient, it could force apart the fastenings that held the costume together and leave the embarrassed actor in a skimpy or abbreviated transformation.

Chapter Eight

The Real Test

Here Comes the Inspector

The early school inspector was expected to visit each teacher's classroom once a year, but as road and transportation methods improved, this figure was extended to two inspections. Most officials were unable to meet these requirements, either because they had too many schools to inspect (about one hundred and fifty on the average) or because of other pressing administrative duties. Bad road conditions and poor railway connections often made it impossible to complete the visits.

Geographically, inspectorates during the 1930s were almost twice the area of the present-day school division or county, and prior to that time were even larger. In 1903, for example, the North-West Territories, which included what are now the provinces of Alberta and Saskatchewan, had eight school inspectors. Their only means of transportation, besides the railway, was by horse-drawn buggy, with a sleigh replacing the buggy during the winter months. It wasn't until about 1918 that the inspectors started replacing their horses with Model T Ford cars.

In spite of all these difficulties, the inspector did his best to appraise the work of each grade in as many subjects as he could in the half day or less that he spent in

In order to cover his area of about eight thousand square miles centered at Bassano, Alberta, in 1913 and 1914, Inspector Milton Ezra LaZerte used a team of horses and a buggy in summer and a cutter in winter. In 1915 the young inspector purchased his first automobile, a Model T Ford.

M. E. LaZerte on his way to inspect rural schools in the Bassano Inspectorate of Alberta in about 1915.

each rural school. He observed the teacher at work, not only in the classroom but also out on the playground. The inspector taught a few lessons himself, and when the opportunity arose, he made a cursory examination of the school building, the barn, the outhouses, the fences, the school yard, and other premises. If at all possible, he also made a short visit to the secretary-treasurer, discussed local school problems with him, and had a look at the financial and minute books of the school district.

After a visit to a school, the inspector made out a report on the teacher in quadruplicate, sending the original copy to the school board, one to the teacher, and one to the Department of Education; the final copy was retained in his own files. He also wrote a supplementary report to the school board indicating any needed improvements or repairs that should be made. The all-important inspector's report recorded information about such things as pupils in each grade, regularity of attendance, punctuality and attitude of the students, the teacher's qualifications and experience, and anything else the inspector considered should be brought to the attention of the local school board, the teacher, and the Department of Educa-

tion. In the main, however, it told how well the teacher was teaching and how well the pupils were learning.

The judgments made by the inspector in these respects were largely subjective, although he also took into consideration the results of the many formal tests that he conducted during the course of his visit. Most officials also placed a good deal of credence on the comparative observations that they made as they went from school to school.

The very heart of any inspector's report was the X that was placed in the lower left-hand corner of the document in one of the squares opposite the ratings: Excellent, Very Good, Good, Fairly Good, or Fair. This was what the school board and the teacher first looked for upon the receipt of the all-important evaluation.

Most inspectors of that day admitted that it was difficult to evaluate the teacher's work accurately. While writing out their reports, they were disturbed by their limited test samples and the short time they had spent in a particular school. Their judgments seemed to be disturbingly subjective. However, it was the decision as to what rating to give a particular teacher that was

Inspector's Report to the Trustees

of his official visit to the _____ *Weise* _____ School.

Date of visit _____ *May 21* _____ 19*20*

SIR,—

In my remarks to the Minister of Education, I have reported as follows on your school property, general standing of the classes and their progress, and the teacher:

Fence _____ *Page wire, Good.*
Fuel shed _____ *Satisfactory*
Teacher's residence _____ *None*
Water supply _____ *Carried in pails*
School garden _____ *none*

Closets _____ *Rather rickety*
Stable _____ *Satisfactory — Roof ridge sagging —*

Interest taken in tree planting _____ *none*
General appearance of grounds _____ *Fairly good*
Schoolhouse _____ *Fair*
Equipment _____
Attendance _____ *Good*
General interest of the Board in their school _____ *Fair*

Repair _____ *Fair*
School records _____ *Fair*
Punctuality _____ *Fair*

General standing of the classes _____ *Backward*

Progress of classes _____ *Fair*

The Teacher. *Mr. Johnston is an earnest, conscientious teacher. His classes are backward but he should bring them along well. I am advising him to insist on greater neatness and thoroughness.*

General Remarks. *The school should be painted outside and kalsomined and brightened up inside. The floor should be painted or oiled. The stable should be painted. The water supply is unsatisfactory. The concrete in the foundation is kracked & should be repaired. Get flag & flag pole.*

I have the honour to be, Sir,

Your obedient servant,

R. N. Dobson

Inspector of Schools.

To _____ *D. Raina Esq.*

Secretary _____ *Weise* _____ S.D. No. *3089.*

really vexing. Whatever was checked off in this decisive "bottom line" might have an important effect upon the career of the teacher.

The book containing the blank forms for the reports had a comprehensive score sheet inside the front cover to assist the inspector in grading a teacher as objectively as possible. In evaluating a teacher, all the official had to do was to study the sample chart; note the range of marks allocated for each of the many traits, characteristics, classroom conditions, and accomplishments; and grade the teacher accordingly. A perfect score in all these teacher attributes produced 100. Then, since each of the five gradings fell within a certain numerical range, it wasn't difficult to assign the teacher whatever rating the total score indicated. Sometimes inspectors found themselves adjusting the score to make it agree with their predetermined rating.

It was not unusual for a benevolent inspector to make a fairer and closer estimate of a teacher's ability by supplementing the official ratings by "plus" categories. One or two inspectors who were not known for their milk of human kindness occasionally introduced a "minus" classification. Can you imagine what it would feel like to be graded a Fair (-) teacher!

Apparently the departments of education must have considered that the addition of the plus categories had some merit, for later report forms appeared with double squares below the Fairly Good, Good, and Very Good ratings. And, presumably not to miss anyone, a Weak or "W" rating was added. Inspectors were now confronted with a very comprehensive rating scale.

The grading of teachers by inspectors was eventually discontinued. The reason given was that it was largely based on the "critical appraisal" method rather than the "professional guidance" technique. In addition, the process was largely subjective and its reliability questionable. It was also at this time that the name *inspector* was changed to *superintendent* in keeping with the new role of these officials.

Not all educators were in agreement with this policy of dispensing with the grading of teachers. They pointed to some merits that the previous procedures had incorporated. The inspector had to be devoted and dedicated in the performance of his duties in order to defend his grading of any teacher, and the terse evaluation never left it to the imagination of the reader to attempt to decide how much emphasis to attach to each of the observations that appeared in an entirely narrative account.

One inspector's report was directed to the trustees with comments and recommendations about school property, general standing and progress of classes, and the teacher. Another form, evaluating the classes and the teacher only, was dircted to the teacher personally.

Teachers have never ceased to wonder why so few school inspectors ever announced their visits beforehand. Usually at the most inopportune time, an ominous knock would sound on the front door and in would march the august gentleman. It would have been appropriate for these inspectors to prefix their greetings to the thunderstruck teacher with, "Surprise!"

The inspectors reasoned that one good way of finding out how well the school was being run was to see it operating as it usually did from day to day. A scheduled visit, on the other hand, would result in preparations being made and give an artificial picture of what the school and teacher were really like. So it was not unusual for inspectors to use various dodges to arrive at school like a ghost, unseen and unheard.

If the schoolhouse happened to be located on a down grade, the scheming official would switch off the motor of his car and coast quietly and stealthily into the school yard. Some inspectors always made it a habit to approach the school from the windowless side, while others had become so familiar with the local districts that they were able to take shortcuts through fields and pastures and arrive at the school unheralded. Another favorite trick was to park the car a short distance from the school behind a clump of shrubs, a shelterbelt, or a knoll and walk the rest of the way. Probably the commonest way was to visit the home of the district secretary-treasurer or the chairman of the school board first and invite one of them to drive him to the school. In this way neither the teacher nor the students would be suspicious of a strange vehicle coming down the road, usually a sure sign of the inspector's visit.

Hence, it can be seen why most communities sided with their teachers in trying to avoid the out-and-out surprise visits. If the district residents had the opportunity, they would usually warn their schoolteacher of any impending visit of the inspector. The grapevine system employed was very effective. Eileen Matthews describes one such method used in her district in an eastern township of Quebec.

The inspector of my childhood was a tiny, hunchbacked Methodist minister named Taylor. He travelled throughout the inspectorate with a white horse and buggy. My father, who was a country doctor, kept an eye out for him on his rounds, and once in a while would report, "I saw Inspector Taylor at Pigeon Hill School this morning," just in time for the teacher to make preparations before the fatal knock came at her door.

Grenville S.D. 3295, in the isolated, hilly country north of Sibbald, Alberta, not only provided its teachers with an unparalleled view of the surrounding areas, but also enabled them to spot the inspector in time to prepare a few things before he arrived. Margaret Wood, who attended the Grenville rural school in the early thirties, reminisces about her school inspectors.

Since the Grenville School was back in the hills, it was seldom that the inspector took the teacher completely by surprise. Generally some wild-eyed youngster would come bolting into the classroom from the little old shack out back with the fateful words, "The inspector's coming!" The teacher would get a mite pale and tremble, things would be straightened up a bit, last minute instructions would be hurriedly blurted out as to how we were to greet Mr.

So and So, and then would come the sinister knock on the door.

The inspector would come up to the front; the teacher would introduce herself and then introduce him to the class. We would all dutifully (if our interpretations of the instructions were right) rise and say, "Good morning, Mr. Aylesworth!" The classes would resume very awkwardly after these preliminaries and continue until recess. After recess, the inspector took over from the teacher and put us through our paces.

We had one inspector who had muttonchops and wore little glasses. He used to peer at us over the rims and scared us stiff. We made horrible mistakes that on any other day would never have occurred.

I was fairly lucky at missing him. Once I had to take lunch to the threshers so I left right at recess time, much to the teacher's disgust but to my relief and pleasure. Another time the cattle got out and I had to take off after them. I managed to get back just as he was leaving. Then there was the time I was taking French and having a difficult time with it. I was at the blackboard writing out some verbs when the news came that the inspector was here. In a flash the teacher grabbed the eraser from me and removed all my work from the blackboard. She shot me back to my desk and told me to get out my literature books and get busy with them. The trick worked, as he didn't have time to check all the subjects and I was good in literature.

Another inspector had a long pet algebra problem he wrote out on the blackboard and asked me to solve. It was supposed to contain a combination of everything I should have known. Ordinarily, I guess, I might have stumbled through. But not being used to working mathematics on the blackboard in front of a class, and the problem not following the usual pattern of the exercises in the textbook, and then being mesmerized by the old boy anyway, I was sunk. My mind went blank, and although the teacher tried to ease the tension by pointing out a few things to me, the solution still didn't come out to what it was supposed

Nothing to smile about in the Minnedosa S.D. (Minnedosa, Manitoba) on this day in about 1910. It was bad enough to have the chairman of the school board visit the classroom, and the inspector showed up at the same time.

to. Near recess the inspector took a hand, and he couldn't get it solved either. He looked at other similar exercises in his briefcase, checking and rechecking them with the one on the blackboard. Eventually it was discovered that he had put in a wrong sign. So much time had elapsed in the meantime that he felt duty-bound to go and work with some other classes. I was glad that it was his mistake and not my lack of ability that had made finding the solution impossible.

We had a teacher once who avoided the inspector for a very obvious reason. She was expecting and definitely should not have been teaching in her condition. Several times school had to be dismissed, and my sister Eleanor and I would drive her home in our buggy, very carefully. However, it always appeared as if this was the time our ponies were eager to travel and were hard to hold. She would yell, "Take it easy! Take it easy!" — which didn't help going down those hills. We always wondered what she was so worried about.

Since this teacher lived not far from the school, she and her husband had worked out

a scheme to negate any plans the inspector may have had to inspect the school or her. The husband, who worked in town, had a good view of the roads in the district and knew the inspector's car. So any time the official's car was headed in the general direction of the Grenville School, there would be no school that day or at least that afternoon. That inspector never did catch up to her.

Not all schemes to prepare for the inspector proved as successful as the ones in the Grenville School. Sometimes such tactics backfired. A. E. Cairns, an early vice-president of the Saskatchewan School Trustees' Association and a former rural schoolteacher, described the following incident in his address to the Alberta School Trustees' Association Annual Convention held in Calgary on February 7 and 8, 1923.[1]

A teacher in a rural district in Saskatchewan prided herself in having an al-

---

1. A. E. Cairns, speech in *1923 Report of the Annual Convention*, 64.

most perfect school if it had not been for two boys who were the bugbear of her life. Speaking plainly, they could have been best described as dunces. In order to deal with them more effectively, she placed them in a special class by themselves. She was always afraid that these two rascals would not only give the school a bad name but also jeopardize her "Very Good" rating on her inspector's report.

She couldn't let such a thing happen so decided to give the two boys some special instructions, as she was anticipating an early visit from the inspector. Fortunately she had taught in this particular school for some time and was very well acquainted with the school inspector and all his classroom idiosyncrasies. Thus, she was able to prepare her two muddleheads with some foresight.

"Jacky," she said to one of them, "you know that the school inspector asks rather general questions sometimes. If he should ask you who made you, you must answer at once and say God made me. I want you to remember that, Jacky!"

To the other lad she said, "Billy, if the inspector should ask you who discovered America, what will you say?"

"I'd say, Sir John A. Macdonald."

"No, Billy, that is wrong. It was Christopher Columbus. Please remember that."

In a few days the inspector arrived, but as it happened, the first boy was not at school that day. Nevertheless, in due course, the class of one was called up. The inspector patted Billy on the back and as had been anticipated by the teacher, asked him, "Who made you, my boy?"

"Christopher Columbus," answered Billy promptly and proudly.

"No, no, my boy," the inspector corrected him. "It was God who made you!"

"You're mistaken, Mister!" Billy replied. "The fellow God made isn't here today."

Departmental Exams

The systematic and efficient manner in which the grade eight departmental examinations were organized, conducted, and marked, and the results released, was fantastic. The task was gigantic and it was accomplished well. Consider all the organization and work that had to be done, much of it confidentially for obvious reasons: setting the examination papers; printing them; sealing them in special brown envelopes, subject by subject, with the required number for each rural school in the province having grade eight candidates; sending these papers to such centers (probably 2,000 of them in 1929) by registered mail or express; compiling a set of regulations for conducting the examinations and enforcing them strictly; receiving and organizing the written answer papers at the examination center; assuring the anonymity of each student's paper by a suitable code system; supervising the marking of the answer papers; recording the results not only for the records of the Department of Education, but also for release in the province's daily newspapers; furnishing unsuccessful candidates with a statement of the marks they had obtained in each subject; and sending a grade eight school-leaving diploma, signed by the minister of education, to every successful student.

The board of trustees in each rural school district was held responsible for all local arrangements in connection with the examinations, including the selection of the presiding examiner. The Department of Education forwarded the supplies required to conduct the grade eight departmental examinations to every rural school: envelopes with attachable identification coupons for the candidates' answer papers; foolscap; blotting paper; and, if necessary, graph or drawing paper. For the presiding examiners, there were instructions and forms for conducting the examinations: the timetable, tally lists, rules, and the presiding examiner's declaration. The safekeeping of the answer papers was also his responsibility.

The rules to be observed by candidates writing these departmental examinations were comprehensive and very strict. Each candidate was advised to make himself thoroughly familiar with the rules, as any infringement could result in the cancellation of his examinations.

(1) Before the commencement of the second day's examinations, each candidate shall, if required, satisfy the Presiding Examiner as to his personal identity.

(2) Candidates shall be in their places punctually at the appointed time, and when the order to stop writing is given, shall obey it immediately. If a candidate be not present until after the time appointed, he shall not be allowed any additional time.

(3) If any candidate desires to leave the examination room, he shall, before he leaves, deliver to the Presiding Examiner his answer papers, and he shall not be allowed to re-enter the room until the expiration of the time allowed for the paper then being written upon.

(4) No candidate will be permitted to leave the examination room until at least one hour has elapsed after the beginning of the examination.

(5) No candidate shall copy from another, nor shall he leave his answer paper so exposed that other candidates may copy from him. He shall not bring into the examination room, nor keep in his desk, any book, notes or papers, or anything from which he may derive assistance. He shall not talk, whisper or make signs to another.

NOTE: In the event of a candidate breaking any of the rules mentioned in paragraph 5, the Presiding Examiner shall, if he obtains clear evidence of the fact at the time, cause such candidate to leave the room at once and shall exclude him from examination in any other subjects.

If, however, the evidence be not clear at the time, or if it be obtained after the conclusion of the examination, the Presiding Examiner shall report the case to the Examinations Board, which, upon approving of the validity of the evidence submitted, shall order the cancellation of the candidate's entire examination.

No candidate against whom is sustained the charge of breaking any rules laid down in paragraph 5 shall be permitted to appear again for examination within one year from that examination period wherein the offence was committed.

(6) During the examination no candidate shall ask the Presiding Examiner for any explanation or statement in reference to any question on an examination paper, nor shall he make any inquiry whatever respecting the manner or order in which questions should be answered. Should an error appear to have been made in the printing of any paper, or in the wording of any question, no attention shall be drawn to it during the time of the examination either by the Presiding Examiner or by any of the candidates. Candidates may, however, at the end of the examination period submit the matter to the Examiner, who, if he considers it necessary, will report thereon to the Examinations Board. A candidate receiving a damaged or imperfectly printed paper shall return it to the Examiner at once.

(7) All candidates shall use only the paper provided by the Department of Education. Candidates shall write legibly and on one side only of each answer sheet, shall use blue or black ink only, shall not underline words with coloured pencil nor use parentheses around words written in error. The name of the subject shall be written plainly at the top of each sheet and the sheets shall be numbered at the top in the right-hand corner in the order in which they are written. *Candidates shall not write their names on their answer papers.* The sheets shall not be fastened together nor shall they bear any marks whereby the identity or the religious or other affiliation of the candidate could be disclosed to the Examiners.

(8) The candidate shall fold his answer paper once across, place it in the envelope provided for the purpose, seal the envelope, write on the outside of the envelope the

CONFIDENTIAL

Number of Papers Enclosed

High School and University Matriculation Examinations Board

EXAMINATION PAPERS

Unit or Subject SOCIAL STUDIES IX

the Presiding Examiner:

_____ S. D., Alb

o be
until
ation
. If
ge is
ch an
have
iding
otify
ly.

*This envelope is not to be opened until the hour set for the examination on the
official time-table, and then only by the Presiding Examiner
and in the presence of the Candidates.*

The sealed envelope in which the confidential examination papers were brought to the school each morning by an official of the local school board. The seal just visible at the right edge of the envelope cautioned: "This package is not to be opened nor the seal broken until the hour set for the examination on the official time-table. If before this hour the package is damaged or mutilated to such an extent that its content may have become known, the Presiding Examiner is required to notify the Department immediately."

subject and grade of examination and, on coupon provided, his name in full, age, school where prepared, address, and the place of writing.

N.B. *Principals are directed to read to candidates the week preceding the examinations the Rules to be observed by the candidates.*

Presiding Examiners will be expected to collect the answer papers immediately upon the expiration of the examination period for each paper, and upon the completion of the examinations, to make a declaration before a Commissioner, Notary Public, or Justice of the Peace that he has not deviated from the official Time-Table.[2]

Local school boards accepted their responsibility for the proper conduct of the examinations in their particular schools seriously and in good faith. Usually a

meeting of the trustees was called and all arrangements completed in good time. Alex Deleff, who attended the Basin Lake S.D. 3703 (Monitor, Alberta), describes how strictly and efficiently the examinations were conducted in the small rural schools.

I can still recall seeing Mr. Archibald Sinclair, the secretary-treasurer of the Basin Lake School during the early thirties, riding to school past our farm for five days each June, dutifully delivering the unopened departmental examinations (much hated and feared by all concerned) to the teacher for each day's scheduled writing. I used to marvel at his punctuality and was greatly impressed by it, as I was with the whole ritual of examinations so carefully attended to by the teacher and the trustees.

2. Department of Education, Alberta, "Rules to be Observed by Candidates," Form 69-22,000, 1939.

134

In retrospect, I think we learned more about the fundamentals of civics and citizenship — duty, trust, and responsibility — by watching neighbors like Mr. Sinclair going about their assigned tasks than from reading from some of the outdated textbooks we had in the school. We held such people in awe, reverence, and respect, and we learned much from them.

In spite of all the Department of Education and the local trustees were able to do to prevent any errors or improprieties in the conduct of the departmental examinations, such things did occur now and then. The sealed envelope labelled the examination papers in one subject would be found by the startled presiding examiner to enclose some other subject when opened before the students seconds before they were to write. Instead of the envelope containing the requisite six papers, maybe there would be only three or four, as somebody had slipped up at the examination headquarters.

The students faced very strict regulations against copying, whispering, using crib notes that had been jotted down on pieces of paper or on expedient parts of their bodies or clothes, employing the moccasin telegraph, or any other such devious devices. The minimum penalty for any of these dishonesties was severe: for the teacher, withdrawal of his or her teaching certificate; for the student, a failure on the examination and for the whole year; for the trustee, dismissal. However, such cases were few and far between. This speaks well for the honesty of children, the teaching profession, and the trustees.

Sometimes the examinations regulations were not exactly broken, but they were certainly stretched a bit. J. E. Birdsell recalls one incident when he wrote the grade eight departmental examinations in the Gore S.D. 650 (Didsbury, Alberta) in 1922.

Four of us, all thirteen- to fourteen-year-old boys, were prepared by a very conscientious and industrious male teacher for our grade eight examinations in his first year at our school. He worked hard and saw to it

that we did the same. When we were writing the geography examination I noticed him, after looking over my shoulder, walk around in an agitated manner. He kept slapping his thighs with his hands, grimacing, and shaking his head. Finally, he went to the front of the room and suggested that we check our papers carefully as one of us had made a serious mistake in the location of a river. I soon found it and set it right. We all succeeded in getting our diplomas.

Madeline Runyan of the Westmoor S.D. 2010 (Punnichy, Saskatchewan) recalls the grade eight departmental examinations with fervor and nostalgia.

Whatever its faults, the grade eight departmental examination system of former years was unequalled as a means of developing the ability to get down to business. It has not been replaced by anything like it as a means of making a pupil take his grade eight seriously. A bond of friendship and comradeship never since known was formed between the teacher and pupils. The problem of discipline now found in many grade eight classes was nonexistent.

When I taught grade eight, we often went back to school in the evening when all was quiet. We were a busy happy family, and these extra sessions to prepare for the departmental examinations are among my most cherished school memories. To this day, my closest friends are former pupils who were in my grade eight classes. We often share the joy of remembering our days in schools now demolished and replaced by ultramodern central ones from which something intangible but valuable is missing.

During the days when the grade eight students wrote the departmental final examinations, the rest of the school was dismissed. So the few grade eights who had to come, like Shannon and Pat in this photograph, found it very quiet except for the scratching of their straight pens. The tension created by the examinations themselves made everyone happy when exam week came to an end.

Bibliography

Athabasca District Local Alberta Teachers' Association. *Clover and Wild Strawberries: A History of the Schools of the County of Athabasca.* Calgary: Friesen Printers, 1967.

Burton, Betty. "Nellie McClung." *Manitoba Pageant* 20, no. 4 (1975): 1-11.

Chalmers, John W. *Schools of the Foothills Province.* Toronto: University of Toronto Press, 1967.

Chalmers, John W. *Teachers of the Foothills Province.* Toronto: University of Toronto Press, 1968.

Delvin, A. R. "Tales of Asessippi — Christmas at Asessippi, 1915." *Manitoba Pageant* 19, no. 2 (1974): 17-18.

Drake, Beverly A. "Edison School District." *Alberta Historical Review* 19, no. 5 (1970): 21-24.

Fair, Myrtle. *I Remember the One-Room School.* Toronto: The Boston Mills Press, 1979.

Goodwin, Theresa. "Recollections and Reminiscences of an English School Marm in Saskatchewan." *Saskatchewan History* 27, no. 3 (1974): 103-107.

Hosie, Inez B. "Little White Schoolhouse." *Alberta Historical Review* 15, no. 4 (1967): 26-28.

McClung, Nellie. *Clearing in the West.* Toronto: Thomas Allen Limited, 1964.

McKenzie, M. I. "School Memories." *Alberta Historical Review* 7, no. 1 (1959): 14-17.

Oster, J. E. "The Prairie Teacher: A Novel Perspective." *Alberta Teachers' Association Magazine* 58, no. 3 (March 1978): 40-45.

Poelzer, Irene A. "Local Problems of Early Saskatchewan Education." *Saskatchewan History* 32, no. 1 (1979): 1-15.

Province of Alberta. *Report of the Legislative Committee on Rural Education.* Sessional Paper 136, 1935.

Province of Alberta. *Tenth Annual Report of the Department of Education,* 1915: 78-150.

Province of Alberta. *Eleventh Annual Report of the Department of Education,* 1916: 46-108.

Province of Alberta. *Twelfth Annual Report of the Department of Education,* 1917: 46-110.

Red Deer District Local Number 24 of the Alberta Teachers' Association. *Schools of the Parklands.* Calgary: Friesen Printers: 1967.

Ronaghan, Allen, ed. *Earnest-Minded Men.* Saskatoon: Modern Press, 1967.

Schultz, Earl L. "Education in the Bruderheim Area." *Alberta Historical Review* 20, no. 4 (1972): 21-27.

Smith, Vivian Martin. *Faces Along My Way.* Saskatoon: Western Producer Prairie Books, 1970.

Tkach, N. "Dirty Thirties, Hard Times of Teachers." *Alberta Teachers' Association Magazine* 58, no. 3 (March 1978): 16-20.

Woywitka, Anne B. "Waugh Homesteaders and Their School." *Alberta History* 23, no. 1 (1975): 13-17.

Picture Credits

p. viii, Saskatchewan Archives Board
p. 7, Glenbow Archives
p. 8, left and right, R. Morrison
p. 9, Ernest L. Larson
p. 13, David Lawrence Irving
p. 15, top, Margaret Rowe
p. 15, bottom, Manitoba Archives
p. 16, top, Mae (Leinhart) Alexander
p. 16, bottom, C. G. Peterson
p. 17, Canadian Pacific
p. 19, Hanna Pioneer Museum, photo by Bob Bellis
p. 20, C. G. Peterson
p. 21, Saskatchewan Archives Board
p. 23, Lloyd D. Staples
p. 26, Hanna Pioneer Museum, photo by Bob Bellis
p. 28, Nina (Pearon) Stewart
p. 31, C. G. Peterson
p. 33, Ralph Ringdahl
p. 37, Glenbow Archives
p. 39, Provincial Archives of Alberta
p. 40, David Bernard Smith
p. 42, top, Hanna Pioneer Museum
p. 42, bottom, Glenbow Archives
p. 44, William Neilson Limited

p. 45, Hanna Pioneer Museum
p. 47, top, Gordon Hay
p. 47, bottom, Saskatchewan Archives Board
p. 50, Provincial Archives of Alberta
p. 51, Helen Northey
p. 52, Madge (Rogers) McCullough
p. 54, Rose (Cotton) Bebb
p. 56, Jill Ebsworth
p. 59, Irene (MacKenzie) McKay
p. 60, Larry E. Helmer
p. 62, Blanche Coultis
p. 63, top, Rose (Cotton) Bebb
p. 63, bottom, C. G. Peterson
p. 66, Leo W. Kunelis
p. 69, Emil Hiltbrand
p. 71, Saskatchewan Archives Board
p. 72, Saskatchewan Archives Board, National Film Board
p. 73, Project Yesteryear
p. 80, Project Yesteryear, Eugene Anderson
p. 82, Sylvia Wick
p. 84, Glenbow Archives
p. 85, Sylvia Wick
p. 87, Helen (Polley) Veno
p. 88, Norine Coad
p. 90, Esther Boulter
p. 91, Helen Northey
p. 93, top and bottom, Verda (Oliver) Gray
p. 96, Sylvia Wick

p. 97, top, S. B. Smith
p. 97, bottom, Rilla Mohl
p. 98, Manitoba Archives
p. 99, Nina (Pearon) Stewart
p. 100, Byemoor History Committee
p. 101, Rose (Cotton) Bebb
p. 103, Verda (Oliver) Gray
p. 104, top, John Stifle
p. 104, bottom, Frank Jacobs
p. 106, Jack Phibbs
p. 107, top, Helen (Polley) Veno
p. 107, bottom, David Lawrence Irving
p. 108, Glenbow Archives
p. 109, Manitoba Archives
p. 111, top, Glenbow Archives
p. 111, bottom, Manitoba Archives
p. 112, Glenbow Archives
p. 113, Manitoba Archives
p. 117, top, Joan (Desilets) Scott
p. 117, bottom, David Lawrence Irving
p. 121, Dorothy Grott
p. 122, Harold Unsworth
p. 123, Marguerite (Hittle) Warner
p. 124, Lorne Proudfoot
p. 126, Dr. M. E. LaZerte
p. 127, Dr. M. E. LaZerte
p. 131, Manitoba Archives
p. 134, Jean I. Benedict
p. 135, Hanna Pioneer Musuem, photo by *The Hanna Herald*

Index